HIDDEN
HISTORY
of the
WISCONSIN
DELLS
AREA

HIDDEN HISTORY
of the
WISCONSIN DELLS AREA

ROSS M. CURRY

THE
History
PRESS

Published by The History Press

Charleston, SC 29403

www.historypress.net

Front and back cover photo,top, by Mary Fairchild.

First published 2010

ISBN 978-1-5402-2097-4

Library of Congress Cataloging-in-Publication Data

Curry, Ross Milo, 1929-

Hidden history of the Wisconsin Dells area / Ross Curry.

p. cm.

ISBN 978-1-5402-2097-4

1. Wisconsin Dells Region (Wis.)--History--Anecdotes. 2. Wisconsin Dells Region
(Wis.)--Social life and customs--Anecdotes. 3. Wisconsin Dells Region (Wis.)--Biography--
Anecdotes. 4. Dells of the Wisconsin Region (Wis.)--History, Local--Anecdotes. I. Title.

F589.W8C874 2010

977.5'56--dc22

2010043798

Notice: The information in this book is true and complete to the best of our knowledge. It is offered without guarantee on the part of the author or The History Press. The author and The History Press disclaim all liability in connection with the use of this book.

This book is dedicated to my loving wife, Sylvia, without whose support and encouragement none of these writings would have been possible.

Contents

CONTENTS

Preface

I was only sixteen years old when I got my first job as a writer, writing sports for the *Wisconsin Dells Events* in 1946. I have maintained some sort of connection ever since.

Since retirement in 1991, I have written a column that first started when I was still employed at the *Events*. It is mostly local history, although I sometimes get into a travelogue or similar subjects.

So when a History Press editor asked Kay James if there was anyone to do a book on local history, she referred him to me. After about six months of give and take, we came up with this book.

It does not contain a lot of well-known Kilbourn-Dells history stories because I have published them before in previous books and they wanted something all new. This is not quite all new, as these stories have appeared in the pages of the *Wisconsin Dells Events* in the past ten years, but it is the best I can do.

Some stories are omitted because I no longer have them in my computer; others don't quite fall under the topic of history.

We hope that future generations will enjoy the effort that went into this book to keep area history alive.

Special thanks to Kay James, Bill Brown, Bud Gussel, Mary Fairchild, Michael Goc and many others for their advice and to the many who contributed to these stories. It is all much appreciated.

Dells Area Is Home to Many Rock Formations

According to some geologists, Wisconsin has at various times been covered by vast ice sheets called glaciers. They claim glaciers gouged out the Great Lakes, with smaller ones digging out Green Bay and Lake Winnebago.

They also say the Wisconsin River ran through Devil's Lake and the Baraboo River flowed into it at Baraboo until it was cut off by the advancing glaciers. This created a great lake that covered most of Juneau and Adams Counties.

The Wisconsin River finally broke through by cutting a new channel through the Dells, and the river took an end run around the eastern end of the Baraboo Bluffs before it once more resumed its journey southwest to the Mississippi River.

When things settled down, there was left a vast array of assorted rocks in the wake of the glacier. These were once islands in the lake, deposits that rode down on the glacier and formations left along the shore where the river cut its way through, such as Stand Rock.

People who live in the western states have been known to snicker at our array of rocks, saying that they have more rocks in their own backyard.

But others, with more than a cursory glance at our landscape, realize that Wisconsin rock formations are unique in the Midwest. No place between the Appalachians and the Black Hills is there the variety of rock formations found in south central and western Wisconsin.

While northern and eastern Wisconsin are relatively flat except for the range that runs through Rib Mountain, our landscape is dotted by such formations as Castle Rock, Mill Bluff, Observatory Hill, Petenwell Rock, Roche a Cri, Blue Mound, Rockbridge and many other places that I probably haven't even seen.

Devil's Lake is an impressive place to visit, with the so-called Devil's Doorway high in the bluffs a favorite, if dangerous, place to have your picture taken.

I think the view from the top of Louis Bluff is just as great, if not more so, as the Devil's Lake view, and it is just as dangerous and difficult

Hornet's Nest. Once a favorite feature at the Stand Rock Landing, it collapsed during a sonic boom over three decades ago. *Courtesy Eric Larson.*

to climb. I have made the climb about eleven times in my lifetime, with various friends and relatives and by myself. I'm not sure I could do it anymore, as the last time I was tired for three weeks afterward. I am told that Tom McBride even rode his horse to the top once. The bluff is privately owned, and it is best to get permission before climbing.

At the foot of Louis Bluff is the grave of Louis Dupless and his family. He was the first settler here and one of the first two or three settlers in all of Juneau County.

Within sight of the bluff is Stand Rock, probably the most famous rock in the Midwest, and numerous other rock formations nearby.

In the Lower Dells, we have Lone Rock, Hawks Bill and several Rocky Islands, one of which is Sugar Bowl Rock. There is also a rock along the railroad tracks where Curry Road went straight east to meet the tracks before I-90-94 cut the road off. We kids used to climb on it and watch the Hiawathas go by. We also called it Sugar Bowl Rock.

But my favorite was always the Hornet's Nest. I never tired of gazing at it when I passed over the Stand Rock Amphitheater trail.

One summer afternoon about thirty years ago, my wife was returning from Spencer Lake Girls Camp with a car full of girls when she heard a tremendous crash. She thought she had hit something. She stopped the car, got out and looked around, but she saw no damage. We later decided that what had transpired appeared to have been a sonic boom.

At approximately the same time, the Hornet's Nest rock formation collapsed and slid down into the valley at Stand Rock. Thus ended my favorite rock formation, but memories and pictures remain, and it will not be forgotten by those who once saw it.

Louis Bluff Was an Indian Lookout

Long before white men came up the Wisconsin River and named the rock formations at the Dells, the Wisconsin River was a superhighway for Native Americans.

The Dells happened to be right near the center of the Ho Chunk territory, so they often passed through. It also was about halfway between the Baraboo River junction and the Fox Portage nearby on the south and the Lemmonweir River junction on the north. So it was a common meeting place for a gathering of the Indian Nations.

These meetings often took place at the Stand Rock Amphitheater, a natural valley just off the river where powwows, conferences and tribal meetings were held.

Nearby, a couple of miles to the north on the river, was an Indian lookout that is now known as Louis Bluff after early settler Louis Dupless. Dupless settled at the foot of the bluffs, where he farmed and served as a raftsman, guiding the rafts through the Narrows in the spring. There were no dams on the river then, and it rose to great heights during the spring thaw.

Frank Weinhold owns the area now, and the house he maintains there once had water up to the first-story windows in 1938, when the Frank Hacker family lived there. The construction of dams at Petenwell and Castle Rock have made such floods a thing of the past.

Above: Beverly and Carl Kraemer enjoy a hike around Louis Bluff.

Right: Part of the rocky trail between the north and south faces on the top of Louis Bluff. *Photo by Mary Fairchild.*

Mary and Jim Fairchild near the foot of Louis Bluff.

The water used to get really low in the summer, too, and I once walked over to Blackhawk Island without getting my feet wet. A cave here, now under water, was also a stopping place for Indians seeking shelter while passing through.

Mary Fairchild, a part-time resident and upcoming expert on Indian glyphs, mounds and graves, wanted to see the top of Louis Bluff lookout and the several Indian glyphs on it.

Unfortunately, I don't know the location of those glyphs. I told her that I would show her the way up, but there was only about a 10 percent chance that a man of my age would be able to climb to the top. I had been up there eleven times before, so I knew how tough a climb it was. This is private property, but I have permission from Weinhold to go up, plus I e-mailed him of my intentions.

I am somewhat amazed that so few local people have ever made the climb; indeed, a lot of people have never even heard of Louis Bluff. I consider the scenic views from the top the best in the Dells.

I picked a nice day, not too hot, sun shining for pictures, and took a few precautions because of my age. I am going to be eighty-one about the time you read this. I took a couple of aspirin, two canes, good hiking shoes, a camera and a couple of candy bars and ate a good breakfast.

We started ascending the bluff near the Dupless graves. It is as steep as at Devil's Lake and has a less defined trail. A recent rain made some of it a bit slippery, and some large fallen trees had to be circumvented.

I stopped frequently to rest but experienced no discomfort. Mary walked behind me, apparently to catch me if I went over backward. She is much younger and more athletic than I am. She has a husband as big as a Green Bay Packer tackle but who can probably block better.

View from the top of the south face of Louis Bluff. *Photo by Mary Fairchild.*

Finally, much to my surprise, I reached the top and showed her the views. "Isn't this magnificent?" I said. "You can see why the Indians used it as a lookout." She agreed.

We took pictures and after a while started down, no mean feat, as one can easily fall down on his face in this place. I think I may be the oldest guy to ever climb the bluffs, but apparently I am no worse for the wear.

Railroad Tunnels
Awe Travelers

After writing stories about local history for more than forty years, I am frequently contacted by people with similar interests. Two of the places I have usually ended up referring them to are Louis Bluff and the old 1857 railroad tunnel under the first railroad tracks. These are places my dad took me to as a boy, and I still enjoy them today.

I had promised Mary Fairchild I would take her to see the old railroad tunnel that she had heard so much about. It was built in 1857 and is as old as the city of Wisconsin Dells. As an Indian mound and artifact buff, she was interested in seeing the famous face on the wall.

The origin of the face is shrouded in mystery; no one remembers it not being there. It is mentioned as early as 1906, and no one knew where it came from then. Most seem to think it was left by early railroad workers, but there is a chance it was created by early Native Americans.

We first obtained permission from the Hagen family to cross their property. The road that serves as their driveway once went all the way from Juneau County Highway J to the river near Blackhawk Island unobstructed. It is now bisected by two railroad tracks, two interstate lanes and two major highways. The road can still be clearly seen by the deep cuts in the roadway.

The author stands near the entrance to the old railroad tunnel, an out-of-the-way tunnel built in 1857 and one of the oldest man-made structures in the area. Before the new dam raised the river seventeen feet, there was a road through the tunnel going to the Dell House on Blackhawk Island.

Mary Fairchild with dogs above the old railroad tunnel.

After the railroad was built, the road then shifted to one that went through the old railroad tunnel until 1895, when the new double tracks, now down to one track, were built through the Upper Dells. Then it was replaced by a road running from Dead Man's Hollow past the Brew barn to Stand Rock Road.

In 1933, the new U.S. Highway 12 was built right through the old riverbed, and the Brew Road was closed.

As we approached the tracks, we came to a rock formation that my mother dubbed Sugar Bowl Rock right beside the railroad tracks. As a kid, I never failed to clamber up on the rock, but somehow it seems like a much longer jump now.

The author silhouetted in the old railroad tunnel.

Trees and fallen timber have obliterated much of the original path. We had some trouble finding our way down to the bottom of the canyon and ended up between the two train tracks instead of on the east side. There is a spring there, and we had to step sharp to keep from getting our feet wet.

We went through the new tunnel first. I had a flashlight as lot of wildlife passes through and I wanted to know where I was stepping (think snakes). When I first walked through it about sixty years ago, there was only a foot-wide path on each side and a murky depth in the middle. It was good thing they paved it or it might have washed out like some other tunnels.

By stepping gingerly over the rocks, we were able to cross the gap to the old tunnel. Water flowed through it, but a sandbar on one side allowed us to walk through.

A number of footprints told us that others had been there before us since the last heavy rain.

A cave in the canyon wall opposite Blackhawk Island.

We also took a short walk up the side canyon where the water washed out the tracks a few years ago. This passes through land my father used to own, very scenic and very beautiful.

It was now time to climb up out of the canyon. I had to go on my hands and knees part of the way but otherwise showed no ill effects.

Once above the tunnel, I pointed out the face on the wall. Everyone is usually a bit awe-struck at this face peering at them out of the rock. If only it could speak. It would tell us of raftsmen, railroad workers, pioneers and perhaps even the Indians who surely must have passed this way.

Robert Allen Was Very First Dells Settler

The first white settlement in this area was in a place no longer inhabited today—Blackhawk Island. Other pioneers, soldiers, lumbermen and raftsmen passed through the area on the river, but Robert Allen was the first to stay.

In 1937, three lumbermen—Allen and Amasa Wilson and C.B. Smith—started north to seek their fortunes in the lumbering business.

The next year, they built a cabin on the south side of Blackhawk Island, which was only an island in the spring before the dams were built. I even walked over to the island without getting my feet wet a long time ago.

Wilson and Smith moved upriver to found New Lisbon, but Allen stayed. Rafting was in its heyday, and the rafts had to be taken apart above Blackhawk Island near Louis Bluff and put back together once the rafts passed through the Dells Narrows, which had a whirlpool big enough drop a house into and could be heard for miles, according to my father, who was the only person I ever met who knew Allen and had been in the Dell House while Allen was there.

Anyway, Allen saw the chance to make money by serving the raftsmen going downriver. He built a larger building, the three-story Dell House. It had sleeping facilities for one hundred men, served food and a strong brew called the "Devil's Eyewater" and furnished gambling facilities and women of the night.

A lot of drunken fights broke out over women and cards, but Allen always said he was proud no one was ever killed in the Dell House. But he wouldn't vouch for the grounds.

Allen was also one of the special pilots whom the raftsmen hired to take their rafts through the Narrows, so business was good as long as the rafting trade lasted. He had several people working for him off and on, including the family of George Orcutt, who stayed twenty-two years and had five children born in the Dell House. Others were McEwen and Hanna Hurlburt, who ran the house after Allen left.

Allen and McFarlane owned the rights to make a bridge across the river at Blackhawk Island. Allen hired an old friend from New England, Schuyler Gates, to build the bridge in 1850, and he collected tolls until 1866, when high water took the bridge out. He also owned a ferry service, another moneymaking business that failed after the new bridge was built at Kilbourn City.

Another public venture was to hold dances at the Dell House. All this came to no avail, as the last rafts went down the river sometime after 1880. My father, who came to the Dells in 1881, remembered seeing them.

Allen finally sold the Dell House in 1879 and, with his money exhausted, went on the public rolls. He lived for a time at the Staples House about a quarter mile from where I was born (also in a house made by the Staples) and probably a little less than two miles from Blackhawk Island, then known as Allen's Island. Two railroad tracks and three roads running through the Rocky Arbor corridor make it seem a lot farther.

In 1887, Bob Allen ended up on the Juneau County poor farm, where he died in 1889. A simple stone marks his grave in a far corner of the Juneau County Home Cemetery. He never married. His gravestone says, "R.V. Allen, 1806–1889."

Allen is remembered for several firsts. He was the first permanent settler on the Wisconsin River north of Portage, the first settler in the Wisconsin Dells School District, the first settler in Juneau County and the first settler in the town of Lyndon.

Louis Dupless Was First Family Man in the Dells

L ouis Dupless was a contemporary of first settler Robert Allen; both settled on the Wisconsin River, and both were raftsmen who guided rafts through the Dells Narrows. There the resemblance stops.

While Allen ran a tavern and bawdyhouse and never married, Dupless was a family man who married not once but twice.

Born in 1820 in France, Dupless left early to join the navy and crossed the Atlantic in time to serve in the Mexican War for an $800 bonus. He gravitated to New Orleans and its large French population after the war and traveled up the Mississippi to the confluence with the Wisconsin River and to the Dalles of the Wisconsin, eventually taking out a claim of 183 acres, including Louis Bluff.

The bluff was an Indian signal point and the outstanding geographical feature in the town of Lyndon. It presented a magnificent view of the Upper Dells, as it still does, and was probably the scene of an ancient Indian battleground, as two different types of arrowheads were found in the vicinity.

Later, the Frank Hacker family lived there for many years, and before the Castle Rock Dam was put in, high water would sometimes come up to the house windows. Now owned by University of Wisconsin professor Frank Weinhold, permission should be obtained before attempting a climb, something I have done eleven times. One man even rode his horse up there, which seems hard to believe.

Louis Dupless's gravestone near the foot of Louis Bluff, named after him. He was probably the second white settler in Juneau County.

Dupless married as his first wife Elizabeth Walklin. They had six children; the first one, Charles, was probably the first white child born in Juneau County.

During the Civil War, he joined the Union army and was wounded at Gravelly Run. After Elizabeth died in 1869, he married Amelia, twenty-six years his junior, by whom he had eight more children. He was well educated, could speak or write in four or five languages and was active in town and county governments.

In 1853, he hired lawyer Jonathon Bowman to turn his squatters claims into preemptive rights. Louis Dupless also did some farming, as well as working on the river, and no doubt got a war veterans pension.

When he died, he was buried beside his first wife at the foot of the bluff that bears his name; his grave can be seen there to this day. Because the graves of him and his wife, their son Charles and their daughter Caroline were sometimes under water during times of flood, the graves were covered by a huge concrete base and surrounded by an iron fence. A public road access leads to the graves.

George Tyler Blood Was First Lyndon Homesteader

I received a packet of information about early Dells area settlers from Judy Blood Soma, the last surviving of the five children of Willard and Jeanette Blood, whom I went to grade school with. It was compiled by Mike Blood, son of Robert Blood, who was in my class for ten years some sixty-five years ago.

Most of this concerns the genealogy of the early settler George Tyler Blood, who took out the first claim in Juneau County in the town of Lyndon in 1848. He came from the old New England family of Nathaniel Blood, who fought in the French and Indian War and had six sons who served in the Revolutionary War, one of whom was killed at Bunker Hill.

They were also members of the famous Green Mountain Boys, as were my ancestors who lived in the area and served in the Revolutionary War as well. It is very possible that they knew one another.

The sixth Nathaniel Blood and his wife, Lucinda, along with their sixteen-year-old son, George Tyler Blood, headed for the Midwest in a wagon train leaving New England about 1835.

The family stopped at Thornton, Illinois, where Nathaniel worked as stagecoach driver for a few years. That is where young George met and married Helen Hurlburt in 1844. The family then moved to Wisconsin, and some of them settled in Poynette, where Nathaniel and Lucinda are buried in the Dekorra Cemetery.

George and his wife made their way up the Wisconsin River to the Dell House on Blackhawk Island, where Helen's mother, Hannah Hurlburt, was already living.

At that time, before the railroad was built, there was a road directly west from Blackhawk Island, traces of which can be seen today. It followed what is now part of Juneau County Highway J and Curry Road but is now also cut off by four roads and two railroad tracks.

About two miles west of Blackhawk Island, George Blood took up the first land to be homesteaded in Juneau County. It was 120 acres on the banks of Hulbert Creek, where a spring that still existed in my childhood no doubt made the location attractive.

This was some seven years before Alanson Holly built his first newspaper business in the woods on the site of present-day Wisconsin Dells. It became the site of the oldest continuously occupied farm in Juneau County and is now the home of Elizabeth Johnson, wife of the late Gordon Johnson, longtime Town of Lyndon chairman.

Helen Hurlburt was a half sister to Dan Carlos Berry, the first settler in Reedsburg, whose colorful background is a story in itself.

The Blood family occupied the farm for over one hundred years. There are still many Blood descendants and other relatives living in the Wisconsin Dells area.

Alanson Holly Settled Here 150 Years Ago

A lanson Holly was not the first in the area, but he was the first to build a house on the present site of Wisconsin Dells 155 years ago.

He built his first house on November 20, 1855. It had a dirt floor, wood heat, incomplete windows and a print shop. This was at the present site of 211 Wisconsin Avenue. He later had a house at 609 Washington Avenue, which the last I heard was still standing and is on the National Register of Historic Places. He also gave a lot to build the Presbyterian church.

Holly was born in 1810 in New York and was an experienced newspaperman when he came to the area. He was the one who suggested the name of Kilbourn City when it was officially named on June 10, 1856.

It was a bitterly cold winter in 1855–56, and no place was it felt more than in Holly's print shop, where three printers struggled to put out the first paper. They heated boards to place on the frozen floor to stand on and dipped their fingers in warm water to keep them nimble enough to set the newspaper one ice-cold letter at a time. This process was still used when I first started out in newspaper work, and I can verify that it is no easy task, even when the weather is warm.

The first paper was "struck" by Holly's son Morton and auctioned off. Bowman and Bailey made speeches, and Bailey paid five dollars for one of the papers.

Much is known about Holly because he printed a lot about himself in his newspaper. He had no neighbors to write about at first, although Joe Bailey built a residence next to him the same year.

The first Daniel Brew lived a mile away, but on the other side of the river. Robert Allen, George Blood and Louis Dupless all were established before them in the town of Lyndon.

And Newport, population nearly two thousand, was across the river not far downstream. Delton had twenty shanties on Dell Creek near the site of the present village downtown. There were Norwegians in Newport also.

It seemed to have been general knowledge in railroad circles in Milwaukee that Bryon Kilbourn was going to bypass Newport and build upstream, and any reasonably educated and intelligent person should have known it. But because Holly was the only one to take advantage of this knowledge, suspicion has never been erased that he was in cahoots with the railroad.

Although he was a member of the Kilbourn Hydraulic Company, he does not seem to have played any larger part than Vliet, Kilbourn, Bailey, Bowman and Stroud in the various misadventures that surrounded the founding of Kilbourn City.

J.E. Jones started the *Kilbourn Events*, later the *Wisconsin Dells Events*, and bought out Holly's old paper, the *Wisconsin Mirror*, so the *Events* can trace its lineage back to that early paper.

Holly was later elected to the state assembly and discontinued the paper for a while. His daughter, Josephine, married Colonel Robert Schofield, and they later owned the Schofield Motel. He was a wounded Civil War soldier taken prisoner at Gettysburg.

Alanson Holly is buried in Spring Grove Cemetery. He still has descendants living in the area.

Don Carlos Barry,
First in Reedsburg

T hree men seem to stand out as early settlers of Reedsburg: Don Carlos Barry, who took out the first claim; James W. Babb, who built the first cabin; and David C. Reed, who built the first village or burg at the Indian Ford on the Baraboo River, always afterward known as Babb's Ford.

Don Carlos Barry, the subject of this chapter, had a colorful background, though a bit confusing. Barry's maternal grandfather, John Rollson, was a soldier who was captured at Tripoli and reported dead. His wife therefore remarried and had three children. When Rollson returned, he heard his wife, Cynthia, was dead, so he, too, remarried and had three more children.

Finally, both second spouses died, and John Rollson returned to his old home to find his first wife a widow. They had a joyful reunion. He also found a daughter by his first wife grown and married to John Barry. Their son Don Carlos Barry was about thirteen and witnessed the reunion of his grandparents.

When Don Carlos was grown, he came to Baraboo in 1844 and built a lumber mill on the river there. A lumber mill needs lumber, so he set about scouting upstream for lumber to use in his mill. He at one time had a claim in Section 7 of Excelsior, near Rock Springs.

In the process of prospecting for lumber, he discovered copper in Section 1 of the town of Reedsburg, on what is now known as Copper Creek. Copper Creek still follows along much of Sauk County Highway H before entering the Baraboo River.

Here Barry staked a claim in 1844 and left until the following spring, when he returned with two experienced miners from Mineral Point. The copper apparently had been carried down from northern Wisconsin on the glacier, and it was soon exhausted after yielding only two tons of ore that sold for ninety dollars a ton and had to be drawn all the way to Mineral Point to market.

Iron mining soon opened up in Ironton, but Barry had enough of mining and moved to Iowa.

Don Carlos Barry's sister came to Reedsburg in 1847, and their daughter, Josephine Shepard, was the first white child born in Reedsburg Township on January 14, 1848. A few weeks later, Don Carlos Barry and his wife had twin girls, Agnes and Alice, the second birth in the township.

While in Baraboo, the Barrys had six people in their household according to the 1842 census. This may have included other relatives as well as their own family.

He also served as a justice of the peace while there. One of the cases that came before him involved two men, named Finley and Barker, who were continually having trouble, so Barry suggested they have a duel since they were both southerners.

It was secretly agreed by the two seconds, Barry and Monet, that the guns be loaded with powder only. After counting the paces, Barker whirled and fired shouting, "You are a dead man!" Finley never even raised his gun but thought he was hit. In a little while, they saw the joke, and it was all settled over a bottle of whiskey. Thus ended one of the first lawsuits in the Baraboo Valley.

James Babb Builds First Reedsburg House

The first settlement in Sauk County was in Sauk Prairie, where the Sauk (French Sac) Indians at one time had a large encampment and many cornfields. When the Indians left, settlers came down the trail from Madison and the Wisconsin River at Fort Winnebago at Portage to start farms. Almost all of the early settlers were farmers or lumbermen.

In 1839, Eben and Roseline Peck crossed the Baraboo Bluffs and started a mill on the Baraboo River. Others soon followed, and a succession of towns sprang up on the Baraboo River as settlers pressed westward.

North Freedom, Rock Springs, Reedsburg and La Valle in Sauk County; Wonewoc, Union Center and Elroy in Juneau County; and Hillsboro in Vernon County were all founded on the Baraboo River. Some became good sized, while others remained sleepy hamlets.

James W. Babb was one of the prominent ones among the early settlers. He was born in Virginia in 1789, moved to Ohio in 1810, returned to Virginia to marry his bride, Rebecca Scarff, and then, after living in Ohio for thirty-five years, suffered financial reverses and so struck out for the new open land in Wisconsin Territory, the Wild West in 1845.

The land around Baraboo was already taken, but he heard of prairie west of Indian Ford in present-day Reedsburg, so he proceeded to go there and build a log cabin for his family, who waited in Ohio.

Don Carlos Barry already had a claim there, but he was looking for lumber and copper. The only neighbors he had were Indians, probably those of Chief A-ha-cho-ca (Blue Wing), who had a camp not far away in Narrows Prairie.

Narrows Prairie had open land, water, a church and a cemetery but somehow never developed into a town.

James Babb never had Indian troubles like some of the settlers did. He shared all he had freely with them and treated them all fairly.

Babb proceeded to build a two-story log house. It was quite an elaborate affair for his day. He was about fifty-five years of age at the time and of robust health. His son John also came along, and they worked together.

A nearby creek, now called Babb's Creek, provided water, and he built a flat-bottomed boat in Baraboo to haul supplies and poled it upriver to Indian Ford, where it was kept to provide transportation during times of high water. The ford, afterward known as Babb's Ford, had a rocky bottom and was only two feet deep during times of low water.

Babb and his son broke seventy acres of land and planted a crop in 1846. Then they returned to Ohio to get their families. Babb sold his remaining property in Ohio and started west in a horse-drawn wagon with his wife, son Phillip and a daughter, Betsy, who was married to a Baker.

He had to stop at Mineral Point, which was then capital of Wisconsin Territory, and register his claim for 960 acres, lest someone jump his claims. They arrived at Baraboo beset by early winter weather and did not get to his cabin until December 8.

Babb wanted to build a dam at this point but lacked money to do it. A man named Reed, after whom Reedsburg is named, later succeeded in doing this.

Babb increased his holdings until he had eighteen hundred acres. In 1860, he and sons raised seventeen thousand bushels of grain, nine hundred bushels of potatoes and 160 tons of hay, an excellent result in the day of horse-drawn farming.

Babb died in 1875, at age eighty-seven, and was buried on his property beside his wife. His son Philip later ran the farm.

David Reed Started the City of Reedsburg

D avid Reed was the last of the three most prominent early settlers of Reedsburg. The burg he started developed into the present city and town of Reedsburg. He himself was not among the first settlers, but the town he started for the employees at his mill bears his name. Reed was tall and slender, with a twinkle in his blue eyes. When someone accused him of breaking the Sabbath by going exploring on Sunday, he said he wasn't going to break the Sabbath, he was only going to bend it a little.

The site of Reedsburg was well known to the local Indians because it was the only place where the river could be forded in the area, being only two feet deep in low water.

It was also the site of an Indian tragedy. Two Indian braves knifed each other to death over the possession of a slain deer not long before white men came. Their relatives buried them on the spot and placed a pole over their graves. The mourners who came often and walked around the graves formed a well-worn path around the pole.

At the site of the Indian Ford, later Babb's Ford, Reed built a dam. The rock bottom of the river here that allowed the ford also made a good foundation for a dam. To attract workers for his sawmill, he built a shantytown for his workers, who were mostly family men with children.

It consisted of five shanties just east of the ford near where Main Street is today. This was about 1844.

The huts were made of tamarack poles that George and Edward Willard had cut on government land upstream. Reed's men confiscated the poles to build their shantytown.

The huts were essentially log cabins with two rooms, twelve by sixteen feet. They had dirt floors and elm bark roofs and were very primitive. The town looked so harsh and barren that one of the first settlers offered the man who drove him there from Baraboo his last three dollars to drive him back. The driver wanted four dollars, so the settler was forced to stay.

In January 1849, there were three feet of snow. Food was scarce, and there was sickness, famine and harsh weather. In the spring, the elm roofs leaked so that the occupants inside the shanties had to hold umbrellas over their sleeping children and set buckets around in the shanties to catch the melting snow and rain leaking through.

The doors became wet and expanded so that they could not be closed at night, and worse yet, if they did close at night they couldn't be opened in the morning. Roads were all mud, but the mill was working sawing out boards. There was no money to pay the workers, so they were paid with lumber, from which they started to build frame houses.

Then the rafters forced the dam to be breached so they could get their lumber through. This shut down the mill and worked a hardship throughout the community. The settlers then turned to making shingles. Austin Seely lost his thumb in the sawmill, so his wife was forced to nail all the shingles on his residence—the first shingles in Reedsburg.

The village was platted in 1852, and in 1856 Reed sold his business. Also in 1856, there were about fifty buildings in Reedsburg, 27 families and 122 people. Reedsburg was well on its way.

Wildrick Grave Is
Historical Attraction

I have made a new friend.

I had heard about Debbie Kinder for some time and know she is on the Wisconsin Dells City Council. Also, I knew her parents, grandparents and assorted uncles and aunts.

I went to school with Bennett Dyer, her uncle, who was the best singer in school. My mother worked for Ruth Dyer, and my father even knew her great-grandfather, H.H. Bennett.

The first time I met Debbie was when she invited me to set up a stand at the Festival of the Dells, where I sold a few of my books.

In the course of conversation, I happened to mention that in 1869 my grandfather's brother, Jim Curry, drove a stage full of men to Portage, where they lynched the notorious desperado Pat Wildrick. Jim Curry said H.H. Bennett was one of numerous local businessmen who participated in the "necktie party." Curry owned a stage line, so he may have been merely a witness to what was widely considered a community effort.

The deputy at the jail put up a big fight, but the men overcame him and went for Wildrick. Wildrick had been in a lot of scrapes with the law before but always seemed to wiggle out of them.

When Schuyler Gates was shot down in cold blood in broad daylight in the area of the Lower Dells Mobil Station while waiting to testify that

Schuyler Gates's gravestone. Gates was murdered by the Pat Wildrick gang in 1869. Wildrick was later lynched by a mob of angry citizens.

Wildrick had robbed him of $3,000 while he was camping on a Wisconsin River Island on the way to Kansas, it was the last straw.

Wildrick took his clothes off and covered himself with grease in an attempt to slip away, but a noose was put around his neck, and he was dragged out to a tree and hanged. Curry said he was dead long before he ever got to the tree. In the morning when it was daylight, the locals found Wildrick hanging about a foot off the ground.

When I told Debbie I know where Wildrick was buried and would be glad to show her, she took me up on it. So one cloudy November day, she arrived with her husband and we did a tour of Old Highway 12 in Lyndon and Kildare, with me being a chatterbox, pointing out the history as we went through.

Old Highway 12 was in existence until new Highway 12 was built through Lyndon Station and Rocky Arbor about 1933. I remember Highway 12 signs on all the culverts in the town.

Lyndon Station was built in the town of Lyndon when the railroad went through in 1857, but the town split up and part of it became Kildare about 1875.

St. Bridget's Catholic Church was near where St. Mary's Cemetery is today. But when they built their new church, it was at its present location in Lyndon Station. The cemetery, of course, could not be moved.

Pat Wildrick's father went to get his son's body in Portage and drove back to Kilbourn, but they refused to let him be buried there. The Catholic Calvary Cemetery was not yet in existence.

So Wildrick's father kept going up Highway 12, now Juneau County J, until he got to St. Bridget's Cemetery. Apparently he was a good Catholic, as they let him bury his son there.

Almost all the graves in the old section of what is now St. Mary's Cemetery are of the early Irish settlers, many of whom have descendants in the area yet. In the new part are a lot of graves of Polish settlers who came later.

We came back to Curry Road as I pointed out where all the early settlers had lived. They treated me to a lunch at Burger King. We all had a good time.

Hubbards Were Among
First Sauk Settlers

O ne of the advantages of being online is that one can do history research from the comfort of a soft easy chair instead of traveling and carrying on a time-consuming correspondence.

Such was the case when, browsing on my computer, I discovered my great-great-grandfather Hiram Hubbard listed in the probate records of Sauk County. He was listed at number eighteen, so he must have been among the very first to have his estate probated. He died in 1868. Also listed at number ninety-five was his son Oliver Baker Hubbard, whom my father often talked about.

Finding the records wasn't easy. I first went to the register of deeds, who sent me to the register of probate across the street. After checking his records, he in turn sent me to the Sauk County Historical Society at 531 Fourth Avenue. I got my streets and avenues mixed up and ended up on the wrong side of town until I realized my mistake and reversed my course. Here the very pleasant lady in charge found the records for me, and I made copies of some of the interesting pages.

Hiram Hubbard was the son of Oliver Hubbard I, a Revolutionary War veteran and descendant of an early colonial family. He had several children whom he left in Chesterfield, New Hampshire, but only sons Oliver Baker, Elias Haskett and Henry and daughter Maria

Elias Haskett
Hubbard—with wife,
Catharine Barringer
Hubbard, and
daughters, Rena and
Belle—was the first
settler in Excelsior near
Rock Springs.

Weatherby followed him to Wisconsin in 1945, when the state was still a territory.

Son Henry later moved farther west and is buried in Canton, South Dakota, but the others remained here at least as long as Hiram was alive. Henry's son Julius was the first man from Sauk County to die in the Civil War.

Hiram's wife, Hannah Archer Hubbard, died in 1849, and her grave was the first in Ebenezer Cemetery, now Pleasant Valley Cemetery on Section 25 in the town of Excelsior in Sauk County. Ebenezer Church was there for a while, but the property was then owned by the Hubbards. The original plat map says O.B. Hubbard donated the land for the cemetery in 1856.

Hiram's son Elias Haskett Hubbard was administrator of the estate. It looks like he and his brother O.B. Hubbard pretty much divided up the estate, although there was one claim from the Weatherby family in faded pencil. Daughter Maria Weatherby died at sea, according to family tradition, probably going to Oregon, where her brother then lived. But she had a son named Albert still around here some place.

The assets of Hiram's estate seemed to be chiefly the northeast corner of Section 26, now owned mostly by the Ahrensmeyers. It also included one steer at five dollars.

Claims against the estate were thirty-five dollars for a gravestone that can still be seen today, a four-foot-high marble marker.

O.B. Hubbard made claims for farming, harvesting, two weeks' board, keeping stock and money lent.

E.H. Hubbard made claims for two years' board for $100, taking care of him with a broken leg for four months for $290, wintering stock and other expenses. He also made a claim for the care of two minor children, his wards, whom I think must have been his grandchildren.

Out of the total estate of $2,330.50, fees were paid for back taxes of about $200.00. It included $1.50 for digging his grave.

The Weatherbys got $870.50; O.B. Hubbard, $819.45; and E.H. Hubbard, $745.00 for expenses, leaving a total of $25.20, which the three families divided equally. The other children apparently did not get anything.

No picture of Hiram Hubbard seems to have survived, but those of the four children who came to Wisconsin remain in the hands of his descendants.

The only thing I learned about Hiram in local history is that he was an eccentric individual. I wonder if I have inherited any of that.

Oliver Hubbard
Settled in 1845

O ne of the first settlers to come to this state while Wisconsin was still a territory was Oliver Baker Hubbard.

Oliver was the son of Hiram and Hannah (Archer) Hubbard, who came to Sauk County in 1845. He was accompanied by his parents, his brothers, Elias Hackett and William Henry, and his sister, Martha. His parents died in Excelsior Township and are buried in Pleasant Valley Cemetery. William Henry moved to Canton, South Dakota, where he is buried. His son, Julius, was the first man from Sauk County to die in the Civil War.

Elias Hubbard moved to Iowa and then to Oregon, completing a lifetime cross-country journey that may be the subject of another story. Martha Hubbard Weatherby died at sea, probably on the way to her brother's in Oregon.

Oliver Baker Hubbard was the grandson and great-grandson of Revolutionary War veterans. His namesake grandfather Oliver and grandmother Lois Baker Hubbard have gravestones in Chesterfield, New Hampshire, where the slate gravestones can be seen with the saw marks still on the top of the stones. They were distant cousins of Roger Sherman, who signed the Declaration of Independence; General William Tecumseh Sherman of the Civil War; Julia Ward Howe, who wrote "The

Oliver Baker Hubbard. He came
to this area in 1845.

Battle Hymn of the Republic"; and former vice president Charles Curtis.
The list fills a two-inch-thick notebook.

The first Hubbards came to New England before 1650 and can trace
their ancestry in the book *1000 Years of Hubbards* to a Viking chieftain and
raider named Hubba.

All the Wisconsin Hubbards settled in the Sauk townships of Freedom
and Excelsior. There, Oliver's parents died and are buried in Pleasant
Valley Cemetery. His mother, Hannah, died and was buried on the farm
in 1849. Oliver donated this plot of land containing his mother's grave to
the Pleasant Valley Cemetery Association in 1856.

Oliver Baker Hubbard was married three times and widowed twice.
His first two wives and three of their five children are also buried in
Pleasant Valley, also known as Ebenezer Cemetery.

He married first Elma Maria Foster. She and their son Cassius
were the first to be buried there. Next, he married Catherine Mary
Howard. They had at least two children, Charles and Jennie, both of
whom died within a week of each other. Oliver was so distraught that

he would take their bodies from their coffins and cherish them if he was not watched.

He also had two sons named William Henry and Granville who are named in his will. I think they were the children of his second wife. I have been unable to learn what happened to them.

After Oliver's father, Hiram, died and his siblings moved away. Oliver returned to Prairie du Sac, where he farmed just south of Badger. The big brick house he lived in still stands.

He married for a third time to Eliza Jane Page. They had three more children—Frank C., who died in infancy, and daughters Julia and Maude. When they grew up, Julia married into the famous North Freedom Hackett family, and Maude married a Converse.

While they farmed at Prairie du Sac, my father used to visit them, driving down there with a horse and buggy, staying overnight and returning to Kilburn the next day. He was my father's favorite uncle, and I am told if my younger sister had been a boy, she would have been named Oliver.

Oliver Hubbard had three hundred acres he farmed there—all prime land, as was his land in Excelsior. When he died in 1895, his daughters moved to Los Angeles, California. A couple times they returned when I was a small boy, and they stopped by to see my dad. Maude even corresponded with me for a short time when I was young.

Oliver was active in the Sauk County Old Settlers Organization and had a poem written in his honor. His home farm is well located, a short distance from Prairie du Sac, and is finely improved. In politics, he was a Republican. He is buried between Sauk and Badger right on Highway 12.

Poem to O.B. Hubbard in Old Settlers minutes

He'll fill you up to your chin,
None can go hungry there,
If you have doubts, just try him once
Then you won't go elsewhere.
You all know O.B. Hubbard

Who came here from old Vermont,
That man I'll bet my boots today
Will never come to want.
He landed on Sauk Prairie in 1845
And when Old Settlers congregate
You'll find him still alive.

Henry and Abigail Barringer
Were Early Settlers

In 1978, I wrote my first book, a two-hundred-plus-page genealogy called *The Forbearers and Descendants of Henry and Abigail Barringer*. It is an imperfect book with quite a few factual errors in it, as I found out afterward, but it is the only genealogy printed on this family history, and it has become known as the "Barringer Bible."

It lists over three thousand names of Barringers and related families, and I had to leave some of them out or it would have been so big no one could have afforded to buy one. Now more than another generation has come to pass, and if anyone were able to fully update it, there would be two or three thousand more names to add at least.

People from nearly every state in the union have bought this book, and I am now down to my last couple dozen copies. When they are gone, there won't be any more.

So every year, two or three families contact me for the latest information, and most of them come to meet me and have me show them where our common ancestors are buried in Narrows Prairie Cemetery between Rock Springs and Reedsburg, where Henry and Abigail Barringer and about twenty of their family are buried.

Henry (Heinrich) Barringer was the son of Peter (Petrus) Barringer and Susan Kuhn, born in 1795 in New York. He lived along the Mohawk

Henry Barringer's gravestone. Early settler Henry Barringer was a War of 1812 veteran who settled on bounty land in Reedsburg. He is buried in Narrows Prairie Cemetery and has thousands of descendants.

Peter Barringer and his second wife, Mary. Peter was the son of Henry Barringer and was one of the first forty settlers in Reedsburg. He was also an early settler in Big Spring.

River and was known as a Mohawk Dutchman, as the Palatine Germans who settled there were called. Peter lived in Rhinebeck until he moved to Williamstown, New York, where he died. Peter was a Revolutionary War veteran who served at the Saratoga Battlefield.

Henry himself served in the War of 1812 at Sackets Harbor and Black Rock. He appears to be the only War of 1812 veteran buried in Narrows Prairie Cemetery, and we placed an 1812 flag marker on his grave on the 100th anniversary of his death on September 21, 1968.

As a result of his service in 1812, Henry was entitled to bounty land. He claimed his just west of Highway 23 some five miles or so south of Reedsburg. His son, also named Peter, apparently came before him, as he is listed as one of the first forty settlers in Reedsburg. This Peter later moved to Big Springs, and Archie Crothers once showed me the house they lived in. Peter married Amanda Ward, daughter of Mahala Case and Samuel Ward, who was also an 1812 veteran and was said to have served with Commander Perry on Lake Erie. He is buried in Big

Spring, and if I can find enough information about him, I will write about them also.

Henry and Abigail had ten children. Calista married in Michigan on the way to Wisconsin; William, Jane and Truman are buried in Narrows Prairie; Susan, Anne, Elizabeth, Catharine and Peter are buried in Iowa; and George is buried on the West Coast. Most of the Barringers' descendants, with the exception of my father's family and one or two others, also moved west, mostly to Iowa and the West Coast. But a lot of the Wards stayed and can be found all over Adams Marquette and Columbia Counties.

Whenever some of Peter Barringer's descendants come to visit, of course I show them the graves of the Wards as well, since they are related to both.

The most recent such family was Ron and Darla Bohn of Iowa and daughter Mandy of Madison. As we drove to Rock Springs, I pointed out the place where my grandmother was born and the school she walked two miles to go to with her older five-year-old brother, crossing a creek on a log. We always stop for the wonderful water at the Rock Springs before proceeding up Narrows Creek to the valley where Chief Blue Wing once lived.

At the cemetery, we found the graves of Henry and Abigail and three of their children, as well as several grandchildren and spouses.

Abigail Hough Barringer came from a long line of New England Yankees that can be traced back to King Edward III. My dad said when she died it was so wet they had to bail water out of her grave before they buried her.

Wards Were Early Big Spring Settlers

Among the first settlers in the Big Spring area were Samuel and Mahala Case Ward. They have always been of interest to me because he appears to have been a friend of my ancestor Henry Barringer, about whom I wrote in a previous article.

Both came from New York for bounty land they had earned for their service in the War of 1812. Samuel's daughter Amanda married Henry's son Peter, and Henry's daughter Jane married either Samuel's son or nephew, as both Henry and his brother had a son named Orson Ward.

In addition, Mahala Case Ward's family and Henry's family both came from Williamstown, New York, which appears to be how the two families became connected.

Samuel Ward was born in 1794 in Delhi, New York, the son of Reuben Ward and Jemima Tiffany of the famous New York glass family.

Mahala Case Ward was born in 1797 in Connecticut, the daughter of Grove Case and Alama Bandell. Case was said to be connected to the well-known tractor family.

Samuel and Mahala's first children, Amanda and Orson S., were born in New York. Ira was born in Pennsylvania as the family moved west. Daughter Sarah was born in Chicago, and Martha was born somewhere in Wisconsin.

Samuel Ward was active in local affairs in Big Spring and donated a log house for a Methodist Episcopal church. He also furnished a log house for a school in what was for a long time afterward known as the Ward School District.

When James Ramsey was named the first town chairman in 1860, Samuel Ward was selected as "sealer of weights and measures," an office I didn't know existed. At the same meeting, Peter Barringer was voted in as one of three constables. Constables were all the law and order that existed on the frontier in those days.

Erwin Crothers says that the farm he lives on was the one that Samuel Ward homesteaded when he came to Big Spring. Samuel died on February 23, 1873, and his son Ira Ward took over the farm. Ira's daughter Julia married Jim Crothers, and they continued the farm.

They were the parents of Archie Crothers, who lived to be one hundred and left the farm to his son Erwin Crothers. Edwin lives on the homeplace today, as his son also farms it.

In 1862, when Indians were on the warpath in New Ulm, Minnesota, Ira Ward was part of a committee to visit Chief Prettyman of the local Indians to urge him to continue to remain neutral in the conflict.

Some of the Indians did go up and fight the settlers, and one returned after being shot in the foot. He was known ever after as "Limpy Jim."

Ira's son Evelyn later took over the Big Spring Mill and ran it for a while. This is the mill that later was run by Emery Lapp. Nearly all of these people are buried in the Big Spring Cemetery.

Sarah Mahala Ward Landt Best Had Exciting Life

O ne of the interesting pioneer stories coming out of this area from around 150 years ago is that of Sarah Mahala Ward Landt Best. She was the youngest daughter of Samuel and Mahala Ward and came to this area with the earliest pioneers. Sarah was born on February 12, 1837, and the family migrated to Wisconsin after the Chicago fire of 1847.

The year 1848 found her living with her sister, Amanda Ward Barringer, one of the first forty settlers in the town of Reedsburg. When Sarah learned her family was in Big Spring, she walked by herself the whole twenty-three miles, crossing the river at Kilbourn by a ferry barge and then walking the rest of the way on trails. She was eleven years old.

When she grew up, she married Jeremiah Landt and had three children. Jeremiah Landt went away to fight in the Wisconsin armies in the Civil War and was gravely wounded. Even though he made it home, he died of wounds, leaving Sarah a widow with two or three children. He was thirty-four years old.

Meanwhile, Socrates Best, a Big Spring schoolteacher, had moved to Texas to teach, taking with him his wife, Ellen Langson, and three children. Socrates Best was Scotch-Irish Protestant, and Ellen was a Roman Catholic. It is said that none of their parents approved of their marriage.

When the Civil War broke out, Socrates' students forced him to either join the Rebel army or be hanged. He escaped and managed to get a position as overseer of a Union army hospital. Socrates said he had $1,400 worth of property in Texas; he left it all and lost it. That would likely be worth one hundred times that much in today's money. His brother-in-law, Ben Langson, was also pressed into the Rebel army and died of disease.

The Rebels told Ellen her husband was dead, killed trying to escape. So she sold what she could, left the rest and started north with a horse and buggy and three children—a boy of eleven, another four years old and a baby girl. They traveled four hundred miles and were all sick when they came to the Union army in desperate straits. Her baby had just died and was buried along the route.

The colonel told her he had a man named Best working at the hospital. She said her husband was dead but it might be his brother.

She was on horseback when Socrates met her and told her who he was. She fainted, and he caught her as she fell.

Socrates got a home for them, and they stayed there for another year, but Ellen eventually died from stress of her illnesses. She also lost another baby.

When Socrates Best's regiment was ordered to move on, he purchased passage for his boys to Prairie du Chien, giving a person all the money he had to see his sons Augustine and William home to his parents in Big Spring.

However, the person took them to Springfield, Illinois, after which he abandoned the boys and absconded with all the money.

Kindly people took the boys in and sent them to a friend in Chicago who took them to Portage, where a man from Big Spring happened to be shopping. He took them to their grandparents.

The little boy was sick a long time but eventually got well. Both Sarah and Socrates mourned their spouses, who were casualties of this long and bitter war.

When the Civil War was over, Socrates returned to his boys in Big Spring. Eventually, he and Sarah Landt got together, each bringing two children to their new marriage. They had four more of their own.

Socrates died in 1896 at the age of seventy-two. Sarah died in 1932 at the age of ninety-five, and they are buried at Prairie Farm, Wisconsin.

Bunce Family Endured
Civil War Hardships

H ester Jane Kyle (Kiel), third child of John C. and Sabrina Kiel, was born on January 1, 1834, in Erie County, Pennsylvania. She either stayed behind when her parents came to Platteville or else returned after her father's death. She married George Henry Bunce in 1855, and their first nine children were born in Erie County. George was usually known as Henry.

Hester could talk German, according to her daughter Susan Bunce, and she said some of the "old folks" spoke such broken English that she could scarcely understand what they said. Her old grandmother, probably John Kiel's mother, used to smoke a corncob pipe. They had to get up in the middle of the night and light pipes for her when she came for a visit.

On Halloween, someone put something above the door, and it fell down on her grandfather. He said, "I helled and helled for my vife but she didn't come."

George Henry Bunce enlisted in the Union army as a private in the F Company of the 199th Regiment of Pennsylvania Volunteers at Meadville, Pennsylvania, on September 7, 1864, and was mustered out with the same rank on September 7, 1865. He contracted yellow fever or yellow jaundice and spent all but three months of his time in the hospital. He never completely regained his health.

His wife, Hester, was home with the children and suffered very hard times. She froze her feet in the winter trying to get in her supply of firewood. The family lived on mush, milk, johnnycake and dried beef.

My grandmother Susan Bunce was the oldest girl and shared a lot of the hardships. When her father was in the army, someone gave her a calf. When it grew up, she said, "Let us butcher it so we will have something to eat." They also butchered a sheep. Some of the beef they dried in front of the fireplace and sent to Henry in the army. Susan, though a very young girl, knitted her father a pair of mittens, and Hester put his initials on it and sent it with the meat. The officers ate the meat and gave Henry the mittens because they had his initials on them.

They raised their own corn and had to carry it half a mile to have it ground for mush and johnnycake. One day, Susan was stirring the cornmeal mush when one of the kids accidentally dropped a candle in it. The heat melted the candle, and they had to throw the whole kettle out, as it spoiled the mush and they couldn't eat it. They had to butcher everything and nearly starved to death.

After Henry Bunce got well enough to travel, they let him go home from the army. His hair was down to his shoulders, and his beard was down to his waist. He was all dressed in rags and could hardly stand up. They said he looked so bad; he was nothing but skin and bones. He was feeble, emaciated and had cramping, chills, diarrhea and a bad cough.

Henry Bunce later got well enough to make the journey to Wisconsin, although it is doubtful if he ever got well enough to resume his former career of logging. The Bunces' experience as pioneers in Wisconsin is the subject of another story. He died in 1876, only forty-three years old, and is buried in Beloit, Wisconsin.

Pioneer Wisconsin Family Lived Among Indians

The George Henry Bunce family nearly starved during the American Civil War. Bunce, known as Henry, came back from the Civil War emaciated and very ill.

By 1870, he felt well enough to journey to Wisconsin, where his wife had lived as a girl and where she still had a sister living in the Prairie du Chien area. Her sister, Ann Elizabeth, married Calvin Neeley and had stayed in Wisconsin when her mother died in 1858.

They came part way to Wisconsin in a covered wagon. At night, Henry and the boys would sleep outside or in some hayloft, while his wife, Hester, and the girls would sleep in the wagon. Their daughter Susan later said they rode ten miles over a corduroy road made of logs—"Bump, Bump, Bump"—in a covered wagon pulled by oxen.

Henry, Hester and Hester's sister settled on a hill near the river, possibly Woodsman, where Myron was born in 1872. At that time, each had a child born in the spring of 1870. The numerous Indians in the area thought they were twins when they played together on the floor.

The Indians of the area were described as "real tough" and used to pester the life out of them, as they were right down the river from an Indian settlement.

Every time they butchered, the Indians wanted the entrails. They would let the Indians know, and they came.

One time, there was a hunched up old Indian woman whom they felt sorry for, and they gave her a good piece of meat. It was freezing, and they went back across the river.

The wolves howled all that night, and in the morning Henry went down to the river to see what was the matter. The Indians had taken the old woman's piece of meat from her and pushed her in the river, leaving her to freeze in the water.

Henry Bunce went over to the Indians and told them to "come over and chop the old woman out of the ice and I won't give you anymore," and he never did.

The Indian women used to come over and beg for things. They would ask for "skash" (squash). The girls tried to play a joke on them by giving them a pumpkin. The Indians rejected the pumpkin, and Hester scolded the girls and sent them back for a squash before they became too agitated.

Once they gave them a squash, and the Indian woman dropped it and it rolled down the hill. She had to chase it downhill and jump in the river to save it.

They didn't keep their doors locked then, and once they woke up in the morning to find three Indian men wrapped in their blankets and sound asleep in front of the fireplace. The Indians always said, "Good friend!"

Sometime later, the Bunces moved to near Rockton, Illinois, and lived on a farm west of Beloit. Henry Bunce once became overheated racing with the kids and caught cold and died on August 18, 1875.

After Henry's death, leaving nine minor children and an unmarried daughter of eighteen, Hester Bunce filed for a veterans pension, but Henry's doctor died shortly after, and she could never prove Henry was dead because the doctor hadn't filed a death certificate. She was forced into two unhappy marriages because she had no other means of support. It worked a great hardship on her family.

Henry and Hester's oldest son, Jacob, named after his father, was hit and killed by a train in Sharon Valley, Illinois. The other children all had productive lives, most living to a very old age.

Susan Bunce Burdick Pioneered in the Dells

S usan Jane Bunce was born on August 23, 1858. She was the oldest girl in the family and shared all the family hardships while her father was away serving in the Union army and then returned home severely ill. She was a small woman, only four feet, eleven inches, and the severe living conditions she endured during her pioneer trek west were typical of those of many families who took the covered wagon route to a new life in the Wild West, which Wisconsin was at that time.

She caught the same illness from which her father died. She was very sick with fever when she heard singing downstairs. It was her sister Emma singing. Her dying father wanted her to sing church songs to him. A couple of days later, he was dead.

Susan heard voices outside and got out of bed to look out the window just in time to see the casket loaded in the wagon. She then fainted away. They came up and found her on the floor. She went back to bed for two weeks.

The Bunce family struggled, although they were entitled to a veterans pension because of Henry's service in the army. They could not prove he was dead. Henry's doctor died shortly after his patient and never filed a death certificate. Susan sent a letter on her mother's behalf in 1879, and as late as 1891, her mother tried to get a pension—but to no avail.

A wedding picture of Charles and Susan Burdick, taken about 1870.

Susan Bunce Burdick was an early pioneer in both Rockton and Kilbourn.

In November 1883, Susan married Charles Burdick. They lived most of the time in a house on the Rock River in Rockton, Illinois. It was right across the river from the paper mill where Charles often worked. In addition, he also worked in a sand pit operating a machine that ground up sandstone to make construction sand. He was an avid outdoorsman who supplemented the family larder with fish and wild game. He had a ferret that would go down a rabbit hole and bring a rabbit up.

Their first two children were Caroline and Mary Amanda. Both died of an epidemic of the grippe in February 1890. A couple of small pictures and a gravestone are all that remain of their memory.

Amos Burdick was born in August 1890. He weighed nearly twelve pounds, and for three days after his birth, Susan did not know anyone. Amos's sister, Sarah Burdick Curry, later said, "Amos was an awfully nice man; he was like me."

Amos Burdick was in the army in World War I and was on a ship to France when they got word the war was over. They turned around and came back.

Julia Burdick was born in 1891 and lived to be 103. She outlived two husbands, being married twice for a total of 75 years. She saw her great-great-great-grandchildren—five generations in addition to herself.

Son Frank Burdick was born in 1893. He once worked at the Dan Brew farm, and he and three others milked eighty cows twice a day by hand.

In 1916, all the Burdicks except Amos came to Kilbourn expecting to improve their fortunes. They acquired the Maine place, just east of the Joe Curry farm in what is now Rocky Arbor. It is now separated by I-90-94.

The place used to be a farm, but after the owner died it was used as a chicken coop, and they had to clean it up before they could live in it. The first winter they nearly starved to death and lived on popcorn and a half gallon of milk supplied every day by sympathetic neighbors, Joe and Ross C. Curry.

Charlie suffered a broken leg when one of the horses he was transporting by train fell on him when the train lurched. Daughters Julia and Sarah had to do the plowing with one horse.

Since then, the fields were planted with trees by the Civilian Conservation Corps in the 1930s, and those trees are now one hundred feet tall. There are four graves on the place, lost to history, belonging to another family who also lost four children to the grippe.

Sunrise in Wisconsin Dells from the author's front window.

September in Wisconsin Dells at the author's home.

January in Wisconsin Dells at the author's home.

Youth paddle a canoe in the old riverbed by Blackhawk Island. Note that none of them paddle in unison.

A scenic side canyon opposite Black Hawk Island, rarely visited.

Mary Fairchild poses near the Face on the Rock above the old railroad tunnel. The face, of unknown origin, has been there as long as anyone remembers.

Left: The view from the base of the north side of Louis Bluff, showing wild rice growing in the river.

Below: Frank Weinhold drives Sylvia Curry around Louis Bluff in his "gater."

This is part of the scenic trails through Rocky Arbor State Park north of Wisconsin Dells. It was built in the former riverbed of the Wisconsin River in glacier times.

Winter scene on Oak Hill Road, west of Wisconsin Dells.

Left: View from the top of the north face of Louis Buff. *Photo by Mary Fairchild.*

Below: Aerial shot of the Ableman Gorge in Rock Springs. The springs are across the road from the tanker, along the river in the lower left side of the picture. *Courtesy Lou Maher.*

When the clipper *Winnebago* used to make night runs on the river, this was a familiar scene. *Courtesy Eric Larson.*

This early scene is probably an artist's depiction, as the river is much wider than this at the Dells. *Courtesy Eric Larson.*

The H.H. Bennett Studio was the oldest photographic studio in America. Civil War veteran H.H. Bennett made the Dells famous with his photos. Today, at right view, it is a state historical society museum. *Courtesy Eric Larson.*

The clipper *Winnebago* lands at Stand Rock. Formerly a paddle-wheeler, it was the largest craft on the river for many years. *Courtesy Eric Larson.*

Charles Burdick Led a Hard Life

The Charles and Susan Burdick family was living on what is now the extreme northwest corner of Rocky Arbor Park. It was then a farm with a barn, a rope-and-bucket well, a house, two large open fields, apple trees and lilacs. A small grave site was also there, left by an earlier settler who had lost four children to the grippe and buried them there. They left for the west and never returned.

Today, everything is gone. The I-90-94 highway took a big chunk of the property. It is unknown if the graves remain or not.

The entrance to the homestead is now a service road to the Rocky Arbor campsite. The only evidence that at least three families lived there between 1850 and 1920 are the lilacs that still bloom in the spring.

In declining health and unable to make a living, Charles Burdick gave up his farming dream and returned to Illinois. The house was torn down to build another nearby, and the homestead was never occupied again.

Charles Burdick lead a hard life. One of twelve children, he never saw the inside of a school after the fourth grade. His father took the boys out of school and horsewhipped them if they did not work on the farm. So Charles plowed every day and forgot everything he learned in school. His wife had to teach him to write his name.

Charles Gardner Burdick with the sand grinder that was used to grind sand for glass in Chicago.

In better days, Charles worked at the Rockton, Illinois paper mill, which was the main employer in the village. It remained in operation well into my time.

A Mr. Manley came from Chicago and asked him if he would like to better himself and boss the sand pit. They ground sandstone and shipped it to Chicago to make glass.

Since Charles couldn't read, his wife, Susan, wrote the payroll names down for him, and he remembered where they were. He put a check if they came to work and an X after their name if they furnished a team. The company would send the payroll from Chicago, and Charles would take it to the bank and put the money in each worker's envelope—that's how he paid them.

When the sand pit ran out of fine sand and closed down, he had to find other means to make a living. The sand pit was on the east side of Macktown, now a developed area.

Stephen Mack was the first settler in Rockton, then known as Macktown. He was also the first settler in Winnebago County, Illinois, and is buried at the old home just west of the stone house, which still stands. It was originally an Indian trading post at the junction of the Pecatonica and Rock Rivers.

Mack married an Indian woman named Hon-no-neg-ah. One day their daughter came to visit Charles and Susan. She was, of course, half Indian. She said her mother would not eat off the table and ate off the floor, and the daughter was a big girl before she ever ate off a table.

Charles's sister, Mary, lived in the stone house for many years. Charles died in 1924, and he and Susan are buried in Rockton.

Tom Ellison Has Many
Area Descendants

Many years ago my dad had a good friend and neighbor named Tom Ellison. Although he lived over a mile away, his land adjoined ours on the north forty.

Once every summer, my dad took me and my sister Eva for a Sunday afternoon walk to see old Tom. He and his wife were pleasant people, and you could see they enjoyed each other's company.

His home was in our school district, and his children walked by our house every day on the way to school. Although that was before my time, they did become lifelong friends with my mother.

Tom's home was on Stand Rock Road right across the road from Hagen's Tavern. Later, his son Elmer owned it, and Elmer's son owns it now.

I always liked Elmer because I was out on a shredding crew one day when it turned bitterly cold, and as I sat on the edge of the wagon and shivered, Elmer loaned me his jacket for the day, an act of kindness I never forgot.

My dad sold his northeast eighty acres to the Ellisons to stay afloat during the hard times of the Great Depression. It included land on both sides of the railroad tracks. It must have hurt my dad to sell the land, as it included some scenic canyons just off the Wisconsin River. I once had some papers about it but threw them away, as I thought it must be a mistake. My dad never said anything about it to me, but my sisters both said they knew about it, as he once owned land back to the railroad tracks. It is also on old maps.

I did learn from these papers that Tom's real name was Tobias Eliassen, but I don't remember just when this transaction took place.

Bergette Gustava Madland married Tobias Bertinius Eliassen in 1895. She was the daughter of settlers who came from Norway and first settled in Newport.

I also learned that she was descended from the same ancestors as two of our best friends in church: Reginald Briggs of Baraboo and Sharon Johnston of Reedsburg. Sharon's sister, Alice Seiler of Portage, has written a brief history of the Madland family in Newport. Some of Tobias and Bergette's children were Elmer and Melvin Ellison, Selma Fisher, Ruth Tumble, Mabel Holden, Tillie Newell and I think Nabors. All were well known in the Dells area, and many descendants live here yet.

Things Were Different Before Kilbourn Dam

M̲y dad used to tell me a lot of things about the river that happened before the dam was built and the water was seventeen feet lower.

He grew up in the gaslight era. There were no car lights, no electric lights, no flashlights and no power hookups. Water power meant a mill turning a water wheel and grinding grain, sawing wood, running a woolen mill or some such thing. The Dells wasn't a very good place to put in a mill like that, but Dell Creek, which flowed through Newport and Lake Delton, had two of them.

There was only one railroad track in the 1880s and most of the 1890s and no running water. On hot summer evenings, sweaty farm boys from lower Lyndon and upper Delton used to go down to Blackhawk Island, which wasn't an island all year round like it is now, and go skinny-dipping to cool off. After they were done, they built a fire in the mouth of a cave, now under water, and dried off before going home in pitch darkness.

H.H. Bennett fought the dam. He believed it would be tragic to flood all the rock formations, which raising the river seventeen feet would do. It also flooded the road that went through the old railroad tunnel, so it is not passable except to hardy pedestrians now. The new railroad had blocked off the passage ten years earlier to horse traffic. Several tunnels under the railroad tracks were flooded, and some are still under water.

The Kilbourn Dam is a prominent Dells landmark. During high water, it is a spectacular sight. *Courtesy Eric Larson.*

It brought the river up to the doorsteps of where the old Dells House had been and flooded a lot of land in the Upper Dells where my father had once cut hay, probably in the vicinity of the Louis Dupless farm. Dupless was a friend of my father.

The new dam tamed the Narrows in the spring. Before the new dam, water rushing through in the spring could be heard two miles away at my grandfather's farm.

It changed the way river traffic operated on the Wisconsin River, too, dividing it into Upper and Lower Dells.

In 1835, the steamboat *Frontier* came up the Wisconsin River as far as the Narrows. In 1850, the *Enterprise* came through the Narrows and beyond. The *Dells Queen*, the *Apollo* and the *Alexander Mitchell*, named after a railroad baron, also plied the river.

A number of small wooden dams had been built on the spot before and were sometimes blown up by raftsmen running lumber down the river. Finally, the raftsmen got tired of it and were going to burn down the village when Joe Bailey faced them off on Broadway and forced a retreat.

Still, my dad remembered the water being so high that he once rode in a tourist boat right over the dam in high water and went all the way to Portage.

On the way home, they got stuck on a sandbar, and all the male passengers had to push on poles to get the craft back into deep water.

Up until this time, a lot of the tourists went up the river in rowboats and canoes. Blackhawk Island and the Narrows are not too far away, being in sight from the Dells. But the high dam paved the way for much larger boats to run the river.

And with larger dams at Petenwell and Castle Rock, I can no longer walk over to Blackhawk Island in the summer without getting my feet wet like I once could.

Lake Delton Has a Long History

Some people think, when they hear Lake Delton washed away, that the whole village is gone. The village of Lake Delton covers several square miles now and probably wouldn't be affected much if every dam on the river went out, but it was real bad for those in the vicinity of the washout.

A lot of people don't realize that Lake Delton was an artificial lake when they first came to the area, but it was right on this site that old Newport flourished before the railroad came in and crossed the river upstream, leaving Old Newport a ghost town in 1856.

Dawn Manor is the only remaining building from this era. It was built by Abram Vanderpoole, a friend of Abraham Lincoln. It has thick walls for Indian protection, is privately owned and is very rarely opened to the public. I, myself, have never had the opportunity to go inside. It was built in 1855.

Vanderpoole was also supposed to have been a friend of Byron Kilbourn, who didn't do him any favors by building the railroad bridge upriver from Old Newport. It is said that Lincoln once visited here, and Civil War troops drilled on the grounds.

Afterward, the building was owned by Newman, Kerfoot and Helen Raab. I think the Raab family owns it today.

Hawk's Bill is a main feature of the Lower Dells. It was named by raftsmen who used to run the river. *Courtesy Eric Larson.*

Some of the very first settlements in the area were at the mouth of Dell Creek, where raftsmen tied up after shooting the rapids in the Dells Narrows as early as 1841. It eventually grew to a village of nearly two thousand people, thirteen stores, three hotels and a brewery.

Newman was a big man, six feet, eight inches tall. He bought up two thousand acres around Lake Delton, investing $1,200,000 in 1920 money.

He hired Ralph Hines, who used a power shovel to build the eighteen-foot dam and make the lake, which was about one and a half miles long and three-quarters of a mile wide. There was a formal opening on June 23, 1927.

Then Newman went down in the great stock market crash in November 1929 and lost all his money and interest in the lake. Hines finished the construction and had a house on the south side of the lake near Dell View Hotel and Golf Course, which was also part of the deal.

Development slowed to a halt during World War II, and we rode around the lake every day in the school bus on the way to school.

After World War II, when the vets came home from the war, development took off again and has been going ever since.

We were a bit surprised to see the stumps still left from eighty years ago. We wonder how many fishermen lost their lures there.

The lake drainage revealed a vast panorama of tree stumps, cement blocks, boat anchors, pails, cans and bottles, as well as sewage from broken lines and other utility ruptures.

The Mirror Lake Dam, which is much older, held, but it was touch and go for a while. Now, Dell Creek flows down from Mirror Lake in much the same channel it did one hundred years ago.

My dad told of high water washing out the bridge and of having to go downstream to pick up the boards and put them back in the bridge so they could drive over.

Everyone no doubt wishes it could be that simple now.

Village of Lake Delton Grew after World War II

I have written about the history of Lake Delton in the past, but this is my personal recollection of it sixty or seventy years ago. We didn't do much shopping in Lake Delton then and mostly just passed through it on the way to Baraboo or Rock Springs.

The bridge over Dell Creek was much lower then but in the same place. I don't know how there happened to be a right-angle turn where the stoplights are. It was always called the Lake Delton Corners. I suspect the original road went straight ahead and connected with the Mirror Lake Bridge a few blocks to the south and west. After all, the village was once called Mirror Lake, and before that it was called Norris after one of its founders.

One of my first memories was of free movies held in the street about a block west of the Lake Delton Corners about 1940–42. I don't remember any of the movies, but there was a skit there once that said women used to wear dresses down to their insteps and now they wore them up to their step-ins.

The cemetery was on the far north edge of town, and there was not much between there and the cabins across from the Deer Park until after World War II. I have been told there were a couple of filling stations, but I don't remember them.

When I rode the school bus the first year it was in existence, we rode over Canyon Road every day, picking up Lucille Baggot and Chick and Donna Kay Patterson. We drove through old Newport past Dawn Manor and what was left of the Purple Grackle every day. The Griffins that are near the stoplights across from the Lake Delton Clinic were over by Dawn Manor then.

We picked up a lot of kids in Lake Delton. I think they included the Deckers, the Giebels, the Alfreds, Marjory Sarrington, Lyle Cole and several others.

Once the bus drove over an electric wire that was down on Canyon Road. Someone yelled, "Are you ready to die?"

I said, "Yes." But I thought he was kidding. Afterward, I heard the school administration gave the bus driver a hard time for doing that.

Parson's Trading Post looked much the same on the outside as it does now. They used to hold Indian dances out in the back. My Aunt Julia, who died about 16 years ago at age 103, said she once lived in that log cabin that sits next to Parson's Trading Post. That would have to have been about 1918.

There was an airport in the area just south of the Lake Delton Clinic. We saw a great air show there about 1936, with a lot of biplanes flying upside down and a man jumping out of an airplane from twelve thousand feet with a bag of flour to show his progress. That was the first time I saw a parachute jump.

Former printer and co-worker Dick Johnson lived in the big house on the hill just north, in back of Pilgrim Drive, for a while. I don't think many, if any, of those roads between Highway 12 and Clara Avenue existed then.

Timme's Mill on Mirror Lake Road was famous for its flour until fire burned it down and destroyed the nearby cantilever bridge, one of only two in Wisconsin.

Sarrington's had a mill over on Lake Delton. I was in this mill several times later when it was a bookstore. It had a lot of original equipment in it yet, but I'm still not sure how they got water power, as it seemed out of place.

There was no actual village of Lake Delton until about fifty years ago, when it was incorporated into a village. Before that, it was always part of the Town of Delton politically.

Hiawatha Drive was always there but didn't have nearly as many homes on it. Co-worker Verne DaWalt built a house there about fifty-five years ago. I used to go swimming in the lake at Reverend Sheaffer's place in the summer, and we skated there in the winter.

And kids come from all over the area to swim at Silver Beach, the area where the lake just washed out last summer.

It has grown from a sleepy hamlet to a fast-growing community in my lifetime.

New Highway 12
Opened Up Development

Before Highway 12 was moved to its present location in 1933, it followed the general direction of today's Juneau County J, only intersecting with present Highway 12 halfway between Lyndon Station and Mauston.

Lyndon Station got its name from being a railroad station dating back to the 1800s. It was actually in the town of Lyndon when the railroad station was built, but when parts of the town branched off into Kildare, Lyndon Station kept its name.

The Lyndon Saint Bridget's Catholic Church had already moved its new church to the village of Lyndon Station after the railroad went through, leaving its cemetery behind on Old Highway 12. It has continued to be used and is now a fairly large cemetery containing the last resting place of many of its pioneer Irish and Polish settlers.

Old Highway 12 was the first paved road in the township. Now called Juneau County Highway J, it branches off old Highway 12 at its junction with Curry Road and reconnects with the new Highway 12 by the Indian Baptist Church.

Old 12 continues from this junction to where it meets Sauk County H near the I-90-94 interchange west of Wisconsin Dells.

There was once a road that went straight east on Curry Road clear to Blackhawk Island on the Wisconsin River. It was abandoned when the railroad cut it off in 1857 but continued about a quarter mile north under the old railroad tunnel where horses and wagons went through. Traces of these roads can be seen today, but the new railroad in 1895 and the high dam in 2005 rendered this road impassible.

Lyndon Road between Lyndon and the Town of Delton was a dirt road at this time, as most rural roads were then, but I remember it because the WPA had a lot of men working on Dobra's Hill to cut it down to size. It was quite high before this. My dad worked on it some to supplement his farm income. He had a big steel dirt scoop—I don't remember the square name for it—that, when pulled by horses, would dig up as much dirt in one scoop as a steam shovel, as they were called then.

I am told the story of one man from whom they wanted to rent horses and scoop but not hire him. He rented them a half-wild team no one could do a thing with, so they told him they would hire him to drive them. The next day he came—with a different set of well-behaved horses!

One fall, a road construction team wanted to leave two of its big steam shovels on our place over the winter. My dad said OK, and they left them on high ground behind the barn.

When spring came, there was a nest of robins in one of steam shovels. My dad took kindly to them, and they waited until the robins had left the nest before driving away the steam shovels.

The new Highway 12 opened up a farm-to-market road to Lyndon Station. My dad drove up there often to sell his cream. They didn't buy milk. There was also a substantial pickle factory near the railroad tracks.

I picked cucumbers all day for ten cents to spend at the free movies in Lyndon Station on the main street in town. Big favorites were Tex Ritter, Jane Withers and Johnny Weissmuller as Tarzan.

I also sometimes got a licorice stick, which until I could no longer eat sweets was always my favorite candy.

Area Looked Different
in the 1930s

O ne of the few advantages of growing old is that one can give a firsthand account of what the area looked like long ago.

Back when I can first remember, the city of Wisconsin Dells ended at the west end of the railroad bridge. It had only recently changed its name from Kilbourn, and for a long time afterward we still got mail addressed to Kilbourn and some addressed to an even earlier name, Kilbourn City.

Dells Park was on the immediate right as you crossed the bridge going north. It had a large Indian settlement in the summer where local Indians sold mostly beadwork and baskets.

I don't remember Stand Rock Road as being paved at this time, but when we reached Brews, instead of turning right under the railroad tracks, the road west kept going straight ahead between the Brew barn and the tracks.

In 1933, the new Highway 12 was completed through Rocky Arbor on its present route. At least three of the men working on the road lived in two campers in a yard all summer. They were the equivalent of today's mobile homes and were almost square, like a little house on wheels. They got water from our pump and probably used our outdoor john. All the cement was mixed elsewhere and carried to the locations in dump trucks. Each of them washed out their trucks every night west of our lilacs, where a patch of cement can be found to this day.

A view of the Wisconsin River and the bridges across it taken from the Riverwalk.

They used a lot of dynamite in Rocky Arbor, and there were dynamite boxes all over. They had to go down twenty feet in Rocky Arbor before they reached solid ground to build the road on.

I remember my first ride on the new road, sitting on my father's lap in the front seat as the construction manager drove us down the road at 70 miles an hour. This was the fastest I ever rode for a long time. Before there were speed limits, I had my wife's Nash Ambassador going 95 once—the fastest I ever rode. One of her brothers had it going 120, I hear.

Water used to go over Stand Rock Road regularly in the spring before the dams were built at Petenwell and Castle Rock, and water got so low in the summer that I once walked over to Blackhawk Island without getting my feet wet.

Brews had the biggest sheep operation in the state for a long time, winning many awards. Before my time, they used to keep eighty cows in that big barn, and my uncle was one of four men milking them morning and evening.

Rocky Arbor was free when it was first made and had a lot of "Wisconsin Wildlife Refuge" signs all around it. Once in a while I still see a rusty sign. The picnic grounds were twice as large as today, but there were no camping sites.

School picnics from all around held their annual outings here. Instead of going up the west side of the Old Riverbed and over the wall to the top, there was a bridge on both ends so one could cross the streambed to the trail on the other side. The first bridge was simply wooden planks nailed to floating logs, no rails. Careless hikers sometimes fell in and got wet. Later, this bridge was replaced with a substantial bridge with rails; it was great fun to race across! I don't know who built it, the WPA or the CCC boys, but the CCC planted hundreds, maybe thousands, of red pines on the west side of the park that used to be farmland. They were six inches tall, and people laughed at them, but they are about one hundred feet high today.

Farm Families Grew Their Own Food in the Great Depression

T he current economic downturn has been described as the greatest recession since the Great Depression of the 1930s. Most of those who lived through it will tell you that the present situation doesn't come close to what it was like in the '30s, when 25 percent of the workforce was unemployed, vast numbers of young men rode the rails looking for work and people left their homes in droves to seek a better life in the far West.

As a small boy then, I didn't know about these things. What I did know was what we had or didn't have on the dinner table.

My father had six to eight cows. He put the milk in the cream separator. I was allowed to turn the crank, and cream came out one spigot and skim milk out of the other. Us kids were always given a cup of warm "new" milk, but I developed a taste for skim milk that lasts to this day. It is still my favorite drink.

We raised lots of potatoes, as most of the Irish families did. In the fall my dad dug them all, and us kids had to pick them up. Then they were poured down the potato chute into the basement. One year we dug one hundred bushels, and we ate them all except for some saved for seed the following year.

No meal was complete without potatoes: boiled, American fried, French fried, mashed or baked in the jackets. Some years we went up to Mike Dineens and dug potatoes on shares. Only rarely did we sell any.

We had a corn sheller that was promised to me, but I arrived one day just in time to see a collector hauling it away. Anyway, with these new combines like Tim Schultz has, it is rare to find a single ear of corn left behind in the fields.

After I shelled corn, I put it in a corn grinder with a sifter on it. As the cracked corn came out, the fine meal sifted into a basin while the coarse cracked corn was fed to the chickens.

My mother used this mealed corn to make johnnycake—cornmeal mush. The mush, when cooled, could be cut into slices like bacon and fried in butter, which was my all-time favorite.

Oh yes! We had a butter churn, too. It looked like a barrel on a spindle that could be turned around and around until the cream turned to butter. We also made smaller amounts in a simple two-quart jar by shaking it. And I drank buttermilk, too, which wasn't bad if enough salt was put in it.

If milk turned sour, it was boiled on the stove to make cottage cheese, which we always called "Dutch cheese." My mother was part Pennsylvania Dutch.

We ate sweet corn and other garden produce in season. We ate field corn when it was in the milk stage, and I couldn't tell it from sweet corn.

In the winter, we got a special treat—maple syrup. When frozen, it was like hard candy, only better. Since moving here, I made three or four quarts of maple syrup one year and couldn't even give it away. Since I can't eat sugar any more, I had to throw it all out.

My mother took peaches, peeled them and put them on a string on the back porch to dry. After a week or two, they tasted like peach prunes. They were delicious and never lasted long.

A couple times my mother made root beer. We stored it in the basement, and it was a special treat. We had a big fifty-gallon crock buried in the ground in the basement where we put our milk and butter to keep it cool. It is probably there fifteen feet under the ground yet. Sometimes we were horrified to find a mouse on the milk jar.

We had a cider press where one put apples and squeezed the juice out. We enjoyed drinking apple cider, which eventually was turned into vinegar. Us kids were never allowed to drink cider after it turned hard. We often wondered why.

Writer Recalls the Great Depression

I survived the Great Depression!

I have had people tell me that I wasn't old enough to remember it, but the worst part of the Depression hit our family in 1936, and I can remember a lot of things that happened that year—and before that.

In 1936, my beloved grandfather Joe Curry died. I spent many a happy moment on his knee. He was always in his favorite chair, which I have restored, and his white whiskers and tuft of white hair on his head reminded me of a blue jay.

In 1936, I was in the first grade. I started in 1935 at the age of five; they won't let you do that anymore. I still remember the first day of school when they were playing King of the Hill on the front school steps.

In 1936, we walked about a mile to the railroad tracks to see the first Hiawatha train go by. I was expecting something slow like a long freight train.

"Here it comes!" Zooooomm—and it was gone in about ten seconds. I was disappointed.

In 1936, we had the hottest summer ever in Wisconsin. It was 114 degrees in the Dells, I think, on July 14. Crops dried up. People left their homes and went west. We sat on the back porch in the evening heat and prayed for rain. After about two weeks, it came.

The summer was preceded by the winter of 1936, which for combined snow and cold was probably the worst I remember. Snow was up to the horse's belly, and we couldn't get in the woods. My dad cut a tree down across the road and brought the trunk into the kitchen, where everyone took a turn on the crosscut saw to feed the three wood stoves in the house.

The Leonard Wharry family had been evicted from their home, and we let them stay in two rooms upstairs until Leonard could build his own home in the spring.

In 1936, the *Wisconsin Dells Events* moved into its new location on Broadway. The owner who moved out was a friend of my mother, and Mother drove our open-air Ford truck to town several times to get hand-me-downs and other things her friend discarded when she moved out from the upstairs. I still have an antique car and a cricket bat someplace I think.

In 1936, we drove to town to see the newest attraction, the "stop and go" light at the corner of Broadway and Superior. They were the first lights in the city, although there were traffic lights at the Lake Delton Village Corner, where cars tipped over regularly because of the right-angle turn.

My sister and I had $25.00 in one of the Dells banks when it closed. Long after, when we were both in high school, I think we each got $4.35 back.

My grandfather moved to Kilbourn and bought a 240-acre farm adjacent to present Rocky Arbor in 1881. In 1892, he borrowed $1,200 from his brother John to finish paying it off. I think that was the only money my family ever borrowed while they lived there.

My dad sold off portions of the original farm bit by bit to stay afloat. Today, there are only seventy-five acres left in the family.

I don't know how they got through the Great Panic of 1893, which was about as bad as the Great Depression. It is hard to believe there was absolutely no national debt then.

We lived by the motto "Use it up, wear it out, make it over, do without."

We never went hungry, although I got awful tired of oatmeal, sardines and condensed milk. But I still like cornmeal mush, especially fried in butter. Some of the old days weren't so bad.

Store-Bought Meat Rare
in Depression

Previously, I wrote about the food we ate during the Great Depression. Or maybe it should be the food we didn't eat. I don't remember my family ever buying any meat until I was about ten years old. It was just too expensive, although very cheap by today's prices.

We picked and my mother canned blackberries, blueberries, strawberries, apples, rhubarb, cucumbers, beets and probably a lot of things I have forgotten.

We picked hazelnuts and ate a lot of greens. Dandelions taste pretty much like spinach, and the whole plant was edible.

Grace Decorah taught us to find Indian food. She went out one day and picked a lot of wild plants that included milkweed and pigweed. When cooked with meat, it was pretty good.

One day she made a stew that we were told was chicken. I found a bone in it that had been broken and healed at a right angle. When I asked about it, my mother hushed me up. I think it was raccoon. My dad was a fussy eater and would never eat wild game. My grandfather on my mother's side practically lived on wild game like rabbit and squirrel, but I could never make myself eat a rodent.

My grandfather also lived on the Rock River in Illinois, and fish was a regular part of the menu. Once my uncle caught a big turtle, and they had turtle soup for a week, but I didn't like it—too wild.

My mother did teach me to fish, and before I got married I used to go fishing every night. Fish from the Wisconsin River had to be soaked in salt water overnight, as the river was much more polluted than it is now. But fish from the lakes was pretty good, better than what could be bought in the store.

A couple times I caught a lot of frogs, and we had frog legs. Not too bad eating but messy to prepare.

In the fall, when the weather turned cold, we often butchered. If it was a hog, it was cut up and salted away in a crock. Salt pork never was one of my favorites. It always tasted more like salt than pork to me.

We raised sheep, and sometimes we butchered a sheep and had mutton. Not as good as pork or beef, but you get used to it if you are hungry enough.

We put the meat in a cold room upstairs with the windows open to keep it through the winter. One year, we had a big January thaw, and all the meat spoiled.

Occasionally, we butchered a beef, especially after we could keep meat in a locker in town. There was no electricity in our neighborhood until I left for school in Madison in 1948.

My dad asked Paul Waltman to come and kill a big bull calf he had been fattening for our winter meat supply. Paul got into the pen with him and hit the calf over the head with a sledgehammer. One blow didn't do it, and that bull calf fought back and nearly pinned Waltman to the wall! Finally, he got in a couple more blows and got the job done, but it was the last time we tried that.

Our main meat supply was "chicken every Sunday." A chicken didn't have to be frozen, salted, pickled or dried and was just the right amount. But I got awful tired of boiled chicken, which I call "water-logged chicken" to this day. My grandfather Curry used to take a chicken by the head and wring its neck, swinging it around like cranking a car. Boy, that was something to see!

Toward the end, we got some commodities: condensed milk, oatmeal, prunes (army strawberries) and sardines (goldfish!).

But one thing I will never ever miss is my mother's burnt flour brown gravy. My wife has strict orders to never ever make it.

Dells Area Was Once
Gang Hideout

The recent discovery of four guns in the murky bottom of drained-out Lake Delton reminds us that this area was once a hangout for Depression-era Chicago gangsters who were fleeing the law and one another.

Gail Jermier, a local historian, and I did a little research on the Tuohy Gang. She shared with me the story about her father, who, as a little boy, would ride along in the ice truck with her grandfather and deliver ice to the many cottages and resorts around Lake Delton and Mirror Lake.

Her father remembers delivering ice to a cabin on Mirror Lake that had an iron gate and armed guards. His father told him many years later that the Tuohy Gang had a hideout there. Having this information about the hideout, she became curious when the guns were found in the dry lakebed. Could they be guns from the Italian and Irish gangs from Chicago?

There was constant gang warfare between the Irish and Italian gangs over the lucrative bootlegging business. They also did a brisk business in gambling, prostitution, robbery and auto theft.

Eventually, the Capone people nearly wiped out the Irish gangs of Bugs Moran and Roger "the Terrible" Tuohy. Nearly all the Chicago gangsters met violent deaths or received long prison terms. During one

The main street of Wisconsin Dells about fifty years ago, looking east on Broadway from the top of the railroad bridge. *Courtesy Eric Larson.*

six-month period, there were over one hundred gang-related deaths in Chicago. That is a lot of hot guns to get rid of.

Highway 12 was the main north–south route in those days, and the fact that the largest still in Wisconsin was only a quarter mile off Highway 12 increased the area's attraction to bootleggers.

Lake Delton had only recently been built by Chicago native W.J. Newman, so of course it was well known as a place to lay low for a while until things cooled off in Chicago.

Roger Tuohy and his four brothers were sons of an honest cop in Chicago. Four of them were eventually killed in the gang wars and another was crippled. Roger made $1 million with slot machines one year when gas was only eight cents a gallon.

The Tuohys did pretty well as long as they had Chicago mayor Anton Cermuk on their side. But Cermuk was riding with Franklin D. Roosevelt in Florida when he was shot much like John F. Kennedy was in Dallas. Most people think the real target was Roosevelt, but insiders say Cermuk was the target of the Capone people in order to isolate the Tuohy Gang.

When Jake "the Barber" Factor was about to be deported because of his involvement in crime, he had himself kidnapped, and it was blamed on Roger Tuohy, although recent historians claim he had nothing to do with it. Jake Factor was the brother of Max Factor, of cosmetic fame. So after a life of crime, Roger Tuohy went to prison for a crime he probably didn't commit.

While in prison in Joliet, Illinois, Roger Tuohy made friends with Basil "the Owl" Banghart. After seven years, they succeeded in an elaborate prison escape with smuggled guns, a stolen car and several holdups to keep themselves financially afloat.

The federal government got involved because the men were draft dodgers. After an extensive manhunt that featured the involvement of J. Edgar Hoover himself, the fugitives were finally recaptured and sentenced to long prison terms.

After twenty-five years behind bars, Roger Tuohy paid his debt to society and was released from prison. Jake Factor was pardoned by President Kennedy, and Tuohy made plans to write a book about his life of crime.

This disturbed many people, who feared being named. After only twenty-five days of freedom, "Terrible Tuohy" met his death in a hail of gunfire.

Could these have been some of the guns found in Lake Delton?

Massive Blackouts Were Once
a Fact of Life

M ost Americans don't realize that electricity is a fairly recent
phenomenon. There are a lot of people living, especially those
who once lived in rural areas where electricity wasn't available at any
price, who can remember life without electric power.

As one of those old-timers who remembers life before electricity, I
looked on with something bordering on amusement at the awful time
people had in the East when they lost electric power. I was watching on
my electric-powered TV, of course. It wouldn't have been so funny if it
had happened to me.

I had lived nearly twenty years before Bob Blood and the old REA
electric company crawled through the attic in our old house and wired it
for electricity. Even then, all we had were electric lights. All the appliances
we now take for granted came later.

I did all my reading and homework by the light of kerosene and
gasoline lamps. Even the schoolhouse was lighted by kerosene lamps high
on the wall, out of the reach of children and seldom used except for
annual meetings and the Christmas programs.

When I was a wee boy, my mother washed clothes on a scrub board,
and it was a huge improvement when we got a gas-powered washing
machine. Clothes were dried on the line and freeze dried in the winter,

when pants and long underwear were brought in frozen stiff and stacked like cordwood. We got ice for our icebox from Kaisers Ice House and then did so only on special occasions. We toasted bread on a wood stove and heated bottoms for the flat iron on the same stove to do the ironing. My sisters put a hair-curling device in the kerosene lamp chimney to heat it up to curl their hair. Sort of makes your hair curl thinking about it, doesn't it?

Our radio was a big morning glory horn connected to a vast phantasmagoria of wires and tubes and powered by a car battery. Our phonograph had a big cylinder disk and was wound up by hand.

TV? What was that? I think it was something we read about in Flash Gordon and Buck Rogers. And even science fiction hadn't thought of the Internet yet.

But Dick Tracy was using something like the modern cellphone, only he had it strapped to his wrist like a watch. Some farmers had gas-powered milking machines, but other farmers like the Brews, who had eighty cows in that big barn, had four full-time milkers doing twenty cows each twice a day. Most farmers only had about eight or ten cows unless they had sons to help with the crops and milking.

We did have running water. I started the gasoline engine, filled a pail of water and then ran, really *ran*, the thirty yards to the house and back again before the second pail was full. But it was the best water I ever drank.

Our freezer was Mother Nature in the late fall, when it was cold enough to butcher and keep meat in a room where it was always freezing. In the summer, we mostly had chicken every Sunday. My mother canned food, something my wife and sister still do.

I also ate dried apples, salt pork (ugh), smoked fish (yum) and pickles preserved in vinegar. It is mostly a lost art now. Butter and buttermilk came from a churn, milk came from the barn, vegetables came from the garden and maple syrup came from the woods.

But I have become so accustomed to my creature comforts that I wouldn't want to go back. I do have to admit that when the power goes out, I still know how to cope. Let's just hope it's not going to be part of our future again.

Direct Descendant of Baraboo's First Family Visits the Dells

I had an interesting visitor last week, a second cousin once removed, Phillip Peck and his nice wife, Nancy. I had not seen him in something like thirty-five years. When he was young, his parents, Vane and Elsie Peck, and my parents were frequent visitors at each other's homes.

Phillip Peck has the distinction of being a direct descendant of Eben and Roseline Peck, who were the first white settlers in both Madison and Baraboo. Roseline is considered one of the outstanding pioneers of Wisconsin and the Northwest Territory.

Since all of this family's living descendants are descended from Phillip's grandfather, William Ross Peck, who was my father's first cousin, they are my cousins as well. And, yes, there are at least ten different people who have had the name Ross in our combined families.

Phil has researched the Pecks back to 1770 in Vermont. A University of Wisconsin graduate and engineer, he worked over thirty years for General Electric. Now that he is retired from this position, he has a little more time for this. But at age sixty-seven, he is still director of business and operations for Clarke Imaging Solutions, Inc. I'm not sure just what that job is, except that it is for a medical supplies company, but he sounds like a busy man yet.

Phil and Nancy Peck pose near the gravestone of his ancestor Roseline Peck in Baraboo. Roseline was the first white woman in Madison and Baraboo.

After we exchanged information and picked out some pictures I later e-mailed to him, we took a tour of Walnut Hill Cemetery in Baraboo, and I showed him where all the Currys and Divines are buried. Of course, they are all related to him as well. Roseline Peck is also buried there.

Eben Peck, son of Moses, married Roseline Willard, granddaughter of a Revolutionary War officer in Vermont. They came to Belmont, Wisconsin, in 1836 and rented a boardinghouse, then called a tavern, from Ebenezer Brigham, the first white settler in Dane County.

Judge Doty, the territorial governor, told them of the new capitol soon to be built on the shores of two lakes in what is now Madison. He asked them if they would go there and operate a boarding home for the surveyors and other officials who would soon be there to build the new seat of government.

The Pecks bought $100 worth of supplies, including a barrel of pork, two of flour and a load of potatoes, as well as other supplies, and started out on April 13, 1837. The second day, Roseline, who was pregnant with her second child, rode all day on an Indian pony to within six miles of the intended capitol, camping in the Nakoma area. A storm with high winds raged all night. The Pecks awoke to the howling of wolves, with two inches of snow on their blankets in the wagon. They broke camp in the dark in a fierce gale.

Their little boy, Victor, then three years old, went with them. He later married Elizabeth Curry, my grandfather's sister.

The Pecks Become Madison's First Settlers

E ben and Roseline Peck became the first settlers in Madison, starting out to the site in a snowstorm. They later became the first white family in the Baraboo Valley.

Abe Wood was supposed to have a house ready for them at the site of the new capitol, and two Frenchmen were engaged to build a cabin, but it was unfinished. Roseline refused to go in until it had a floor and was plastered. When Governor Doty saw that this was finally done, he insisted that Roseline move in and play hostess to "Hotel Madison" on Lot 6, Block 107, of South Butler Street. This was then on the lakeshore but is now a considerable ways inland due to the filling in of the lake.

The Pecks moved in and bought a load of hay and thirty pounds of feathers to put in bed ticks and set themselves up for business. The nearest settlement was twenty-five miles away, but frequent visitors from Fort Winnebago (Portage), Galena (Spring Green), Mineral Point, Fort Howard (Green Bay), Fort Crawford (Prairie du Chien) and Juneau Town (Milwaukee) kept the Pecks busy.

On September 14, 1837, Eben and Roseline's daughter was born in the log cabin, the first white child born in Madison. She was named Wisconsinia Victoria Peck (her middle name after the new queen of England), but she was always known as Victoria Peck.

Roseline Peck was an excellent violin player and gave dancing lessons three times a week—a touch of elegance on a rough frontier. In addition, she was a good cook, being noted for her turtle soup. The turtles were caught in Mud Lake and frozen solid, and they rattled around like stones in the food cellar. In the spring, some were surprised to see some of the turtles thawed out and crawling around in the cellar. She also liked canoeing on the lake, but the government kept stealing the boats.

Eben Peck complained about having to "be a servant to everyone." As justice of the peace, he officiated at the first marriage in Madison on April 3, 1838. He married Abe Wood to a daughter of Chief De Kaury (Decorah). He also added to the cabin and built several other buildings. Eben suffered from an eye infection and went to Fort Winnebago at Portage, but he returned without being treated due to the large number of soldiers being treated there.

Finally came the straw that broke their backs. After clearing eighty acres, breaking sod and putting in fences, buildings and other improvements, Judge Doty showed up and said he had sold them the wrong piece of land and they would have to move off.

Disheartened by what Roseline later called "this piece of crooked business," the Pecks left Madison and never recovered a cent for all their hard work on the property there.

Roseline Peck Becomes the First
White Woman in Baraboo

E ben and Roseline Peck became the first settlers in Madison only to have their claim jumped by Judge Doty, the territorial governor, no less.

Disheartened by what Roseline called "this piece of crooked business," Eben Peck set out to explore Baraboo Valley on the north side of the Baraboo bluffs in 1839. His partner was James Alban, discoverer of Devil's Lake and head of the first white family in Sauk County. Alban was later killed in the Civil War while commanding a regiment of the Eighteenth Wisconsin volunteers at Shiloh. (My wife's great-grandfather fought at Shiloh with the Eighteenth Wisconsin.)

Peck and Alban staked out a claim straddling the Baraboo River at the lower oxbow. The land was not opened up for settlement yet, so the Indians were not very friendly to these squatters. Peck called the little settlement that grew up around his mill Manchester.

Shortly thereafter, Peck, his brother Luther and Roseline decided to see the claim for themselves. They drove a carriage to the foot of the bluffs and then had to follow an Indian trail over the bluffs into Baraboo Valley. The trail was marked by blazed trees, and the brush was so thick that it had to be cut so Roseline could get through on her horse, riding in a man's saddle, to this valley no white woman had seen before.

William Ross Peck I, grandson of Eben and Roseline Peck, the first white family in Madison and Baraboo.

The Indian villages were gone, and Roseline wanted to see the farmland on the north side, so she swam the river with the men, getting a "thorough soaking" in the process.

Peck started the first school in Baraboo. E.M. Hart of Sauk Prairie came to Baraboo to become the first schoolteacher. Hart's marriage to one of his pupils was the first marriage in Baraboo.

In 1844, Eben Peck left for Oregon, claiming to be seeing about government offers to settlers. Nearly all of Peck's party was massacred by the Indians, and it was long supposed that he perished with them.

Afterward, reports started to trickle in that he had remarried and had five or six children, but it is really not known what finally became of this early Wisconsin settler.

Widow Peck had her claim jumped once again by one Chauncey Brown, who took over her business and home. Roseline had spent several hundred dollars improving the property and once more had nothing to show for it.

Roseline then moved to her property north of the river and lived in a shanty shack with her children until a more substantial house could be built. It must have been quite a substantial house, as she lived in the upper part and used the lower part for balls, public meetings, etc. She also took in settlers until they got settled because she was glad to get neighbors.

Roseline Peck lived in Baraboo for sixty-seven years and was a much-respected citizen. She cared for the sick, even setting bones. She noted that no one ever died in Baraboo Valley until after the doctors came.

In her later years, Roseline lived with her daughter Victoria, who was married to successful lawyer Nelson Wheeler. These three are buried on the same lot in Baraboo Walnut Hill Cemetery.

Victor married Elizabeth Curry, and after serving in the Civil War, he later became owner of the old *Sauk County Democrat* newspaper. He then owned and operated a leading hotel in Madison and is buried there.

Victoria had no children. Victor and Elizabeth had a son, William Ross, and a daughter, Anna. We were frequent visitors at Anna's home in Rock Springs when I was a small boy.

All of Eben and Roseline's descendants are from William Ross Peck. They are scattered across Wisconsin and some are out of state.

There is a historical marker on the site of the first settlement in Madison, and there are Roseline, Victoria, Wheeler and Elizabeth Streets still in Peck's addition in Baraboo.

Joe Curry Was Early Settler

My grandfather was born on June 3, 1849, in Richland, Ohio. He passed away in August 1936. There are probably fewer than ten people still alive who can remember him, all of us old.

To me, he was a loving grandfather with a snow-white beard and a tuft of hair that stood up on the crest of his head that always reminded me of a blue jay. He liked to hold us little kids on his knee while we chattered away to him.

Some fond memories of him were renewed when we ran across a "Statement of Personal Property" signed by him for his personal property tax in the town of Lyndon in 1911. He declared fourteen head of livestock and fifteen pieces of machinery for a total of $561. The same property today would be worth over $100,000.

J.B. Curry's full name was Joseph Blue Curry. Joseph Blue was a friend of his father who worked with him in the plastering and stone mason trade.

Joe Curry decided not to follow his father's footsteps. Farming was where there was money to be made then, and he purchased a farm on the hill on the east side of Rock Springs (then Ableman) and then west of the twenty-five-year-old village of Kilbourn City in 1881. All the buildings at that scene of happy memories are gone now except the remains of a granary. Lilacs my grandmother planted bloom in profusion every spring and continue to spread. An apple tree, a few plum trees and a cedar tree still remain from this early settlement. But the memories linger on, and this ancient tax statement brings them back to life again.

Horses were the most valuable things my grandfather had. They were assessed at $100 apiece and accounted for more than a third of his personal property value. The ten head of cattle including two heifers, and two calves were about all a family could handle in the days before tractors and milking machines. I know they had chickens, geese and turkeys, too, but there is no place for listing them on the statement.

They had two wagons, sleighs and buggies. Every farm had to have a wagon and usually a bobsled for winter use. The remains of the old bobsled still sit in the grass on the old farm, all but the iron runners returning to the dust they came from. I know they once had a buggy, too, because my dad used to tell of driving one to a farm near Sauk City, where his uncle Oliver lived, and driving back the next day. The yellow brick house where he lived still stands on Highway 12 near Badger Ordnance Works.

I was a big kid before I knew my dad had a grain binder. That was because he stored it in Alfred Hendrickson's shed most of the time. A corn binder sat out behind the garage, and I spent many an hour sitting on it and fancying myself cutting corn, row after row. I later did do this, but I was riding Frank Feyen's binder, and it was pulled by a tractor, not horses.

The hay mower was only valued at five dollars; they are worth a lot more as antiques now, and my brother-in-law has one just like it sitting in his lawn in Oak Creek. That was the most fun of any of the farm equipment I ever operated.

I still have the hand plow that I walked behind, mile after mile, just like Hamlin Garland in *A Boy's Life on the Prairie*. I am still hoping to fix it up and put it in my yard someday.

The gasoline engine was a one-cylinder, hit-and-miss engine. I will always remember the "chatter-chatter-bang, bang, bang!" the engine made as it picked up steam for a big log. I later remade the entire wood saw rig myself.

My mother sold nearly all these things for a fraction of their value, not knowing their real worth, but memories remain and can only be told when written on paper, and that often ensures that they will remain forever.

Hackett Family Settled
North Freedom

H ave you ever been to Hackett's Corners? I have. Never heard of it? For about the first twenty-five years of its existence, that was the name of present-day North Freedom.

The Hacketts were the first and most prominent residents of the village, but in 1871, a man named Bloom succeeded in having the railroad depot built on his property and promptly renamed the village Bloom after himself.

This proved unsatisfactory, and it was changed to North Freedom since it was in the northern part of the town of Freedom.

For a short time, it was called Bessemer after the man who learned to make steel out of iron, but that ended when the iron mines gave out in the LaRue area. The town of Freedom itself had also been called Brooklyn, Eagle and Prairie du Sac.

The first settler in the present village of North Freedom was Samuel Hackett in 1849. At this time, the area was covered with hardwood trees like maple, and a spring nearby made it an attractive site on the Baraboo River. All the available land around Baraboo was already taken, so Samuel Hackett headed west.

In the spring of 1849, Hackett came with two covered wagons, one pulled by two milk cows, to the town of Freedom. He had eleven children. The mother and four small children stayed at a neighbor called Archibald Barber's while Samuel and the five big boys cleared the land.

By fall they had a good house with a brick fireplace and a large sleeping room upstairs. They also had a good supply of vegetables, nuts, fruits, wild game and even cranberries found near the river fifteen rods downhill. This was a safe distance from spring floods.

There were no neighbors closer than four miles. The only school was also at that distance. They still had to grub stumps for cropland and collect a supply of wood to heat the house for the winter. During this process, they made maple syrup. It took forty gallons of maple sap to boil down to one gallon of maple syrup.

In the spring, they added a kitchen to cook for their large family and also a milk house and blacksmith shop since Hackett was a blacksmith by trade.

They had a threshing machine in 1854, the kind powered by horses. For fifteen to twenty years, they did all the threshing in the area. The area also prospered from hop raising for a while.

Several sawmills flourished while lumber lasted, making lumber for homes, ties and fuel for the railroad and wood for barrels.

For a time, there was an iron mine in the LaRue area, and a spur railroad was built to this location. They ground up the iron ore to make red paint for barns and the railroad cars. This spur line is the one that present-day Mid-Continent Railway Museum operates. There was also a cheese factory for a time in 1882.

Samuel Hackett's sons and other relatives soon filled up the location. Still, there were only twelve to fifteen houses in 1872, when the railroad went through. Hackett died about two years after the railroad came and was buried in Ebenezer Cemetery northeast of town, since the North Freedom Oak Hill Cemetery was not in existence yet. Ebenezer Cemetery is the old name for Pleasant Valley Cemetery, where my great-great-grandparents and other assorted relatives are buried.

The village was plotted in 1873 and incorporated into a village in 1893. It is still a charming place in which to live.

Colonel Ableman Settled Rock Springs

I have always had a soft spot in my heart for Rock Springs, the scene of many memories from my childhood.

Not only was it the birthplace of my father, but also, for the first ten years of my life, we had relatives living there, and every two weeks in nice weather we rode over there in an open Ford touring car, later remodeled into a truck, to visit my father's cousins and have dinner with them.

The early history of Rock Springs is largely the history of its first settler, with the square name of Stephan Van Rensselaer Ableman. He was born on December 23, 1809, in New York and had served for a time as a colonel in the New York Militia. He was known ever afterward as Colonel Ableman.

Ableman died about 1880, but not before my dad, then a small boy, met him. Dad said Ableman was a big man; sources say he weighed 325 pounds.

Ableman worked in New York as a carpenter before coming to Wisconsin in 1850. His family stayed in Baraboo while he explored the countryside for a good place to settle.

He moved up the Baraboo River to the Upper Baraboo River Narrows. Here was the confluence of the Baraboo River and Narrows Creek. It was a good place for water mills, sawmills, gristmills and other types of

Author Ross Curry points to a plate stating that the Van Hise Rock in Rock Springs is nearby.

mills using water power. He was also absolutely convinced that Byron Kilbourn's railroad, now moving west from Milwaukee, would have to pass through here.

Like the citizens from Newport, Ableman was misled, but he persevered, and in 1872 he saw the Chicago and Northwestern line go through right by his front porch.

Ableman was postmaster, farmer, miller, hotelier and real estate agent, among other things. Being postmaster meant that the railroad brought a large box of mail to his house a couple times a week, and the citizens came and helped themselves.

My great-grandfather, with the unlikely name of Elias Haskett, Hubbard was one of the first settlers in 1852. My grandmother, Calista Evaline, was born there in 1853 and, in the forty-six years of her life, never got more than forty miles from her birthplace.

Sometime about 1872, she married my grandfather, Joseph Blue Curry, and my father was born in 1874. I can still locate at least three houses connected with the family. There were a lot of German people there then, and there was a German Baptist and German Lutheran church. My grandfather Joe could speak German with the best of them.

Ableman had formed a group called the Air Line Company to bring the railroad to Rock Springs, so named because of a good-sized spring that still flows year round on the west side of town.

So when Ableman succeeded in getting the railroad to pass through in 1872, the appreciative citizens renamed the village Ableman in his honor, and it was so called until 1947, when it was changed back to Rock Springs.

In 1857, he hauled timber from Baraboo for a sawmill. Then, in 1861, he hauled machinery for a gristmill from the new railroad depot at Kilbourn City over bad roads to the site.

There was so much quarrying in the area that the bluffs around the river do not look the same as in Ableman's day. There was so much dust in the quarry that the husband of the cousin we went to visit who worked at the quarry died of the dust in his lungs.

But the springs still remain the same, although they have been moved to the other side of the road. It is still a great place to quench your thirst.

Writer Recalls Fond Childhood Visits to Rock Springs

S ome of the fondest memories of my childhood seventy or so years ago were our trips to Rock Springs, then known as Ableman. Rock Springs lies on the Baraboo River where it goes through the gap in the West Baraboo Bluffs at its junction with Narrows Creek. My dad knew Ableman himself and described him as a big three-hundred-pound man.

The reason for going there was my grandfather's niece, Anna Peck Pierce. Anna was the granddaughter of Eben and Roseline Peck, first settlers in Madison and Baraboo on her father's side, but I didn't know that until long afterward.

My most vivid memories of going over there were in my dad's open-air 1914 Ford Truck. He bought it new as a touring car, but when the top wore out, Clarence Utter made a box for the back and it became a truck. My dad drove, my grandfather sat in the middle and my mother sat half turned around watching me and my sister sitting on boxes behind the front seat. There was no driver's side door. If we made the slightest move, my mother made my dad stop the truck. We were never in any danger, as he only drove about twenty miles an hour anyway.

Dogs would chase the truck; chickens scattered across the road. Once a dog jumped up and nipped my grandfather's coat sleeve when he sat on the outside.

We took various routes over there. One of them was from Highway 23 around a wide, sweeping curve to a junction with the road to Reedsburg a couple miles west of Rock Springs. They were all dirt roads then, and I remember this one because it had a grass strip down the middle of the road that the car had to straddle.

Just before we reached the railroad tracks there was a house on the right side where my dad always said his mother was born. She was three years old when she and her five-year-old brother walked two miles north to school, crossing a creek on a log. The school is still there as a private dwelling.

A couple of times the Baraboo River was over the road west of Rock Springs, and we had to turn around and drive into the village from the other side. In Rock Springs, we always stopped at the springs from whence the village got its name. It used to be on the other side of the road. For a long time, after the Pecks moved away, we would still stop there for picnics sometimes.

Once on the way over, we took a goose along for dinner. On the curve over by Lake Delton, the goose got out, and I can see my mother yet chasing it through the fields. They wouldn't let me help, even though I *knew* I could have caught it. This gave a new meaning to the phrase "wild goose chase." Everyone enjoyed the goose dinner, except the goose.

Anna Peck Pierce's house is still standing. It has a half circle set of upstairs windows in front above the porch. At that time, it had a well-furnished double living room in front where us kids lay on the floor and looked at the "funny papers." In back were the kitchen where we ate and a cistern that pumped rainwater into the house for washing. We were never allowed upstairs. Out back there was always a beautiful garden with lots of flowers.

When Anna's brother, William Peck Sr., died, Anna raised his three children there. They were Bill, Vane and Vida Peck. Vane used to come visit my grandfather Joe Curry when he was a boy. He always spoke of his uncle Joe in the most glowing terms. When his parents came to get him, he went out and hid in the haystack so he wouldn't have to go home. Vida was still there when Anna Peck died in 1939, and we attended the funeral in the house.

Since all of Roseline and Eben Peck's living descendants are through their grandson William Peck Sr., they are all also related to us. We have kept infrequent contact with the family over the years, and I have written about them before. Now, Eben and Roseline's great-great-grandson Phil Peck of Waukesha is writing a thorough genealogy of this family.

The Old Kilbourn Co-Op
Is Remembered

I noticed there was some digging and grading going on at the site of the Old Kilbourn Co-Op Exchange south of the railroad depot. I haven't learned what it is for at this writing, but whatever develops, I doubt it will be as interesting to a small farm boy as the Old Kilbourn Co-Op Exchange was.

Two of my dad's old friends worked there. They were, as I remember it, Ernie Storandt and Louie Mess. Delbert Morse, who worked in the office, was later to be my neighbor. These men were always the face of Kilbourn Co-Op Exchange to those who did business there.

The exchange had a tall grain elevator, like we see by the railroad tracks and like a lot of the farm towns do on the prairie to the west of here. Feed was ground here right up to the last.

I first remember doing business there when they were buying potatoes and loading them into boxcars from the west side of the tracks back in the early 1930s. We also sold calves, lambs, wool, chickens, eggs and probably a lot of things I have forgotten.

I know that when we needed a little grocery money, we could take a cord of wood down and sell it back in the days when a lot of people burned wood. Wood was sold by weight, and after we unloaded my dad's car, he was careful to tell us kids to stay in the car so that the co-op wouldn't be paying us for our weight also. I understand some people tried these tricks to gain a little more money at the expense of the co-op. There was a huge pile of wood on the site of the southwest corner of the Washington and Superior Streets intersection.

Some farmers sold grain here, but we seldom had any to spare. Selling chickens was always interesting because of all the commotion they made. They had a little fenced-in coop where all the chickens went. I am not sure if they were sold by weight or number.

On the south end of the main line of buildings we sold eggs sometimes. Egg money didn't amount to much. We bought all sorts of stuff here like egg mash, oyster shells, fertilizer and salt blocks.

A lot of farmers had corn shelled here and left the cobs. We could go in and shovel as many cobs as we wanted into gunnysacks and take them home to burn. We discovered there was a lot of corn that went through with the cobs, and we used it to feed our chickens.

The Kilbourn Co-Op Exchange was the lifeblood of farmers for a long time. My brother-in-law, the late Gordon Johnson, said that they had to close down when the railroad raised the rent from $75,000 to $750,000 a year, as I recall. A lot of people thought that some local businesses considered the ramshackle collection of buildings a blight in the city and were behind the forced removal.

At any rate, that chapter is past and a new one is begun. May the next chapter be as exciting as the old one.

Free Street Movies in Lyndon Station Remembered

I am not much of a movie guy. I never paid to see a movie in my life until videos came out with closed captions, and I have seen only about a dozen of these.

Movies had a bad name in some circles in the old days, even though the worst of them were probably better morally and ethically than the best ones now.

Even so, there was a period in the summers before World War II when they showed free movies in the streets of Lyndon Station every Friday night in the summer, sponsored by the local merchants. They had big crowds, and people brought benches and blankets to sit on and prayed it didn't rain.

They usually started out with cartoons. I remember Felix the Cat being a favorite. Another popular feature was *Our Gang*. It is a sad fact that only a couple of *Our Gang* actors lived long enough to draw social security. Several of them died violent deaths.

I remember one time they had a Laurel and Hardy "picture show," as movies were often called. All through the show, they were talking about reincarnation, with Hardy saying he wanted to come back as a horse. Finally, in the end, they are in a car accident, and Hardy sprouts wings and flies off into the sky. Later, Laurel walks dejectedly down the road when he hears a voice calling his name. It is a horse, and Laurel goes over and says, "Gee, Hardy, I'm so glad to see you."

Cowboy movies were favorites, and the number one favorite was singing cowboy Tex Ritter—even more popular than Gene Autry, another contemporary western singer. Ritter's son John was the star of a popular sitcom until he died in 2003.

There were also advertisements for Dodge cars doing all kinds of mobile acrobatics that often left the car pretty dinged up. But it was fun to watch.

Along toward 1942, there was a lot of footage taken by the United States Signal Corps of World War II, which was then in progress. I remember seeing the Battle of Midway.

Always there was one intermission when they stopped the show before the main feature, and we were all encouraged to patronize the sponsors of the movie. Being near the end of the Great Depression, there wasn't a lot of money to go around. My dad did business mostly with the creamery and pickle factory, which wasn't open at night. But I remember ads for Pat Brunner and the Laabs store.

There was usually a serial going on with one chapter each week. One was an airplane show called *The Black Ace* with a lot of World War I airplane action. We named our black cat the Black Ace, and she was around a long time.

Jane Withers was another favorite. I see her once in a great while on old movies on TV. Most of the other actors and actresses of that day are long dead.

All movies were black and white. My favorite character was always Tarzan, as played by Johnny Weissmuller, an Olympic swimmer. I was so fond of him that I tried swinging through the lilacs—with very mediocre success.

As suddenly as it started, it all stopped. I don't remember seeing any free movies after 1942. There was no gas to get there, and sometimes not even a car to go in. The free movies were over and finished, but the memory lingers on. I never drive by Lyndon Station's main street without thinking of then.

Kurth Family Had Large Columbus Brewery

A while back, I wrote that I would have another brewery story coming up. This concerns the Kurth Brewery, founded in 1859 in Columbus and continued by family members until Prohibition was passed on January 16, 1920. It then sold soda pop until the repeal of Prohibition in 1933.

Some say Prohibition forced it to close, but it sounds to me like a huge fire that burned the entire block on which the brewery was located was more instrumental in its closing.

The Kurth name is still prominent in Columbus, and thousands of references on the Internet refer to the network of souvenir stores, tourist attractions and so forth that have grown up around it.

It all started in Germany, where Christian Kurth, then spelled Curth, was born in 1800. He and his wife, Catherine Reinhardt, had four children born in Witzenhausen, Germany: Heinrich John (Henry), Christine, Dorothea and George (my wife's great-grandfather).

Christine married A.F. Schwartz, and they are buried in Columbus. Christian and Catherine Kurth are buried on the same lot and have their names on the same stone.

Dorothea married Johannes Schojahn. George, the youngest, married Maria Plunz, who was born on the ship over here. She was from Prussia, now part of Poland. He is famous for his diary of the Civil War and is buried in Whitehall.

The Kurths appear to have come to America in 1848, arriving in Baltimore. Henry Kurth married Fredericka Homeyer. After their marriage in 1850, they moved to Lewiston, Pennsylvania, and lived there until 1859, when they moved to Columbus, where they lived with her sister, the above-mentioned Dorothea Schojahn, until they got settled.

Henry Kurth was a brewer by trade and arrived with a four-barrel brewer's boiler.

In 1865, Henry built a large brick brewery at a cost of $4,000 on Ludington Street in southwestern Columbus, on a lot the size of a block that he purchased when he first came to Columbus.

A year later, he made other improvements and put in a larger boiler. His plant now had a capacity of sixty barrels a week, although the demand only reached to about three hundred barrels a year. By 1914, it was making one hundred barrels a day.

Kurth Mansion in Columbus. Henry Kurth came from Germany and started a famous brewery later destroyed by fire. His home today is a historic site.

Henry Kurth died in 1882, and his wife died in 1902. They are buried in Columbus Hillside Cemetery, and their gravestones are written in German. They are about one hundred feet up the hill from where his father, Christian Kurth, is buried.

In 1904, Henry's sons and grandsons incorporated the Kurth Company Brewery with a capital stock of $400,000. His sons John and Christian Kurth II built the large mansion seen in the picture that today has become a tourist attraction.

The frontage on Ludington had three hundred feet and nearly as much in back. Several large brick buildings were from three to six stories high and all connected. John H. Kurth was president of the Columbus plant, and his brother Christian was in charge of a malt house in Milwaukee with a capacity of 3 million bushels.

Today, all that remains is a small brick building on the northeast corner. There is a bar in it, but it is only open for special occasions like weddings and meetings.

A disastrous fire destroyed the rest of the plant in 1916. But the Kurth name lives on. The location still belongs to the descendants of the original founder, and the homes they built are museums open to the public on occasion.

One direct descendant, Captain John "Hans" Kurth, was appointed to West Point by Herb Kohl and was killed by a roadside bomb in Iraq. He was the twelfth man from Wisconsin to die in the war and is buried in the same cemetery as his ancestors in Columbus.

Biggest Dells-Area Brewery Was a Moonshine Still

I received a letter from Edward Enz a while back. He is the son-in-law of my former lawyer, Bob Dougherty, and a friend of former co-worker Bill Brown.

He enjoyed the story of the Hoffman Brewery in Old Newport and asked me to write something about the three moonshine stills that used to be on old Highway 12 during Prohibition.

I am not sure if they are the same three that I knew about, as there were a lot of these stills in Juneau County. Prohibition was over by the time I was old enough to know anything about it. I only know of them by hearsay.

One of the stills was on the Evans farm just over the Sauk County line in Juneau County. This was just across the old Highway 12 from us, although our farm's houses were on opposite ends of the properties. Another was where Dale Gray lives, across the line fence from us at that time.

A third was about two miles up the road at the Cary Bonfoey farm. My dad found out about this accidentally when he went up and tried to buy some hay from Bonfoey. It turned out there was a still under the haystack, and Bonfoey got angry at my dad because he thought my dad was working for the revenuers.

My folks didn't drink moonshine but had a live-and-let-live philosophy. My mother was present at the Gray farm when a raid was made once, and she told about it later. There was a false step on the stairway that lifted up to go into the basement where the still was. When the sheriff was looking around, the kids sat on this step so no one noticed it was loose. I later lived one year in this building when I was first married, and the remains of a big metal tub where the moonshine was once made was still in the basement.

Lyall Wright, the infamous boy sheriff of Juneau County, is said to have called up many of the stills before he raided them to let them know he was coming. He was ousted by Governor Zimmerman for violating the Federal Prohibition Act.

Later, he was acquitted on a murder charge and then sentenced to prison on a bank robbery charge in which a teller was shot. I think the teller's name was Hale, and I used to talk to him when I worked in Mauston sixty years ago.

Wright's Brother Neil was mayor of Mauston at that time, and another brother, Leland, lived about a mile from me in Lake Delton. I bought a garden tractor from him with a wagon, plow, cultivator and drag that I still use.

The still on the Evans place where Dean Dorow now farms was said to be the largest in the state of Wisconsin. The barn has since burned down. According to the *Events* last week, Henry Evans did not know there was a still there, but you can't prove that by me.

There was a big raid on that place in 1928 with some gunfire, but this must have been the gang that couldn't shoot straight, as no one was hit.

Eugene Blood was the only living witness to this, as he saw men running across his father's fields with federal agents in hot pursuit when he was only eight years old. Four men were arrested. Al Capone also supposedly did business here.

A story in the December 6, 1928 *Events* tells of the still, which cost $75,000 to make in 1928 money and had a capacity of one thousand gallons a day at $6 a gallon.

The premises were full of copper pipes and containers that the feds promptly punched full of holes.

I doubt if the Hoffman Brewery was ever this big.

Panic of 1893 Strikes
Western Settlers

Augusta, Montana, August 30, 1893. From a letter to Kilbourn by Rena Hubbard Johnson.

There isn't much news here, it is the same thing week after week and I suppose it will be year after year unless someone should strike a rich gold mine. There are always lots of prospectors and claims staked off in these mountains.

What do you think Congress will do about silver? The panic has struck the west in earnest and a number of the banks have failed, among them was where [husband] Bert did business and all of our money is in there. To be sure it is not much less than $1,000 but we have less than $5 in the house and it will have to do until the cattle are shipped sometime in October.

A rancher sold his entire stock of horses, some worth $40 to $60 for $10 a head. A man is coming to cut our oats, 10 or 12 acres, for $20. He will have to take his binder apart besides coming 15 miles to get here.

It has been hot, hotter, hottest and also the reverse, I have never seen such weather in all my life, and I am old you know, 21 a short time ago. Last spring nothing grew until July. It was so cold the 13th of August that I kept fire all day besides keeping the doors and windows closed.

We did have tomatoes large as tea cups, green, for tomatoes were never known to get ripe around here. The range is all dry and grain not watered has dried up.

Last year we got 300 bushels out and I think we will get 600 this year, it is about ready to cut.

Prairie fires have been all around us. Some sports from up around Great Falls set fire to brush piles just to see it burn and the boys worked for 8 days and nights with other men around here before it was stopped. Somewhere back in the mountains there is a fire burning and it is quite smokey here.

Were any hops raised there [Kilbourn] this year and if so could you send me 3 or 4 pounds? It is quite expensive to buy yeast here when we eat so much food, 9 big loaves every week.

Wolves are very numerous and doing a great deal of damage to stock growers. They have killed 5 or 6 calves for us and one cow. The wolves found the cow when she was calving. A near neighbor had 17 calves and the wolves killed all but two.

I raised about 60 chickens this year, got lots of eggs, more than I can use and there is no market for them.

Still haying, have about ten more loads to get. It has been so windy that lots of days nothing could be done.

My flowers, what few I have, are looking splendid. I haven't had time to look after them, it takes all my time to do my work and watch the baby. She is just learning to walk and is always into everything.

You tell me not to raise a family but you don't tell me how to keep out of it. I believe it would kill me off if I was as prolific as some of our relatives. Yet baby is a great comfort to us, we think she is the nicest baby there ever was.

About the Author

Ross M. Curry was born on November 13, 1929, in a farmhouse at the height of the Great Depression. He attended rural schools and was an honor grad of Wisconsin Dells High School before attending what is now Madison College.

He worked as a printer and later as a writer for the *Wisconsin Dells Events* for forty years, the longest anyone ever worked for a newspaper in Wisconsin Dells. He has been partially deaf since a childhood illness but learned to communicate by lip reading.

He married Sylvia Phillipson on April 6, 1963. They are parents of a son, Ross P. Curry, and a daughter, Laureen Hunter, and have five grandchildren. He was an active church worker for most of his adult life and taught Sunday school for fifty-five years.

He presently writes a column for the *Wisconsin Dells Events* and another for his church newsletter. He is a former member of the Dells Historical

Society and the author of nine books on genealogy and local history. He has written over one thousand published articles.

Ross's grandfather moved into the area as a baby in 1849, and his father knew all the earliest settlers in the Kilbourn-Dells area. His grandfather's sister married the son of Eben and Roseline Peck, first settlers in Madison and Baraboo, and all of their descendants are related to him.

CPSIA information can be obtained
at www.ICGtesting.com
Printed in the USA
LVHW051249220723
753110LV00041B/1